THE WINNING MINDSET

How To Live Up To Your Potential

Emmanuël Stockbroekx
Vice Olympic Champion
Worldchampion

10-10-10 Publishing

The Winning Mindset: How To Live Up To Your Potential

Stockbroekx, Emmanuël.

THE WINNING MINDSET: How to Live Up To Your Potential

Copyright © 2019 by Emmanuël Stockbroekx

ISBN: 9781091144590

First 10-10-10 Publishing paperback edition August 2019

Publisher
10-10-10 Publishing
Ontario, Canada

Contents

*I dedicate this book to every person
who wants to make something out of this life and make this
world a better place by starting with themselves.*

*I dedicate this book to my dad.
You came back from hell, and the devil didn't win.*

*I dedicate this book to my mom.
You are passion and love.
And I love you. You are the best.*

Foreword

Would you like to know what goes on in the mind of a world champion and Vice Olympic Champion? In *The Winning Mindset*, author Emmanuël Stockbroekx has had the courage to write down what is going on in his heart and mind, after seven years of playing at the international top. He and his field hockey teams, KHC Dragons, HC Bloemendaal and the Red Lions, have become authorities in the field hockey world.

Emmanuël has been dedicated and committed in achieving the top with these teams, and in achieving his dreams and his goals. And now he wants to share with you what it takes.

He shares what he thinks is very important in his life, and what moments, decisions, and ways of thinking have determined his success. He believes strongly that in sharing this he can help you become better, and have the confidence to achieve your dreams and goals in every field you are passionate about.

I have known Emmanuël since 2018, and have witnessesed his journey from an unhappy, unbranded athlete, to a speaker, author, coach, as well as a happy athlete. He has been invited as a keynote speaker at a joint venture of Cipal and Schaubroeck, to speak in front of one thousand people. He played in front of an Indian crowd of 18,000 people, has played for the national team for 7 years, won a silver medal at the Rio Olympics 2016, and won the gold medal at the World Cup 2017 in India.

Achieving greatness by doing what you love can truly impact the world for the better. If you are looking for the book that will help you set on the trajectory to success, you have picked up the right one!

Raymond Aaron
New York Times Bestselling Author

Kind Words from My Coach

It's very interesting what Emmanuël is doing. He's putting the bar higher in his sport every day. His mindset and commitment on and off the pitch are rarely seen. He had an urge to put his ideas on paper and share them with the world. What he learnt and how he strives to live a better life. He learned to overcome failure and fear. It's amazing how eager and enthusiastic Emmanuël is to make an impact in this life. He knows that life can give you challenges. Can give you obstacles to overcome. He knows in order to achieve a goal or dream, you need focus and you need a lot of help. Through this book he wants to help those people who are also struggling to go after what they want to reach. For many this may assist you through your journey as Emmanuël walks you through his journey.

The process that started with writing his book is wonderful. After reading this book you can understand more what it takes to achieve your goals and dreams both on and off the pitch. What you can expect and what things are important to grow. Asking the right questions. Believe the right things. Living without fear and going for you dreams and goals takes courage. You will have a lot of naysayers. People who bark at you. Who give you names. Who don't want you to succeed but when you do succeed, will still say that you were lucky. It takes grit. It takes sacrifices, tears, heartbreaks; it involves taking big risks, taking big responsibilities. It takes commitment. It means discipline, hard work and determination. It requires self belief. Emmanuël wrote on his wall 'Yes I can'. It's interesting to see inside the life of Emmanuël and how he wants to write history for his small but brave country.

The magical mindset is not only for sportsmen, but also for business. As his father is a businessman, he has become familiar with the hard, competitive and greedy environment of businesses. Emmanuël has found that the secret lies in rising above the rat race. To transcend the lower circles of life and live an abundant, fulfilling and happy life true to your heart and feelings. The many areas where Topsport and business are similar. The ups and downs. The way you have to be flexible for unseen challenges and changes. To expect the unexpected. To tackle fear of failure and fear of success. To go above success. To not be afraid to go further than your success and not settle down. To have a plan or a vision for your team and yourself. To make tough decisions. To take the initiative. To follow your gut even if it means you don't know where it will bring you. Or it means hurting people. Work hard in the dark. Moments where no one believes in you but you. Moments where the only good things you'll hear are good things you say to yourself. Moments where you are alone sitting on your bed not seeing it. Not feeling it. Where the enthusiasm and excitement that you had in the beginning of the endeavour will fade away and you feel like giving up. And you'll feel like a dried up reptile in the desert. Going from one fata morgana to the other and not believing that you will reach the other side. Emmanuël has felt these things and he came on the other side.

The dream of becoming World Champion and Olympic champion is one for many young boys and girls who dream to be on that stage. In this book 'the magical mindset' he gives these young people an insight in what to expect when going for that dream. Or what mindset you need to have to make a dream become a reality. It's different from any other things you will hear.

Emmanuël really wants to make the Belgian brand a world known force in the field hockey world. He wants to show that even a country as Belgium with its complex politics can overcome his history and rise above the past to create a better future.

The energy Emmanuël can bring is big. He dares to dream big but is ready to put in the day to day hard work. He knows great things start with small actions.

Shane Mcleod,
Coach - Belgium Red Lions.

Acknowledgements

I want to thank my **Family**, and specifically my parents, who gave me *love* and always *believed* in me even when no one did. Through their love and belief, I was able to go after my dreams and goals, and keep going after the many setbacks I've encountered.

I want to thank:

Raymond Aaron, for guiding me in the process of writing a book, and for encouraging me every step of the way. His high energy and wisdom made it possible for me to complete my book so quickly.

Family Dreesmann, for giving me my first hockey stick, for introducing me to the field hockey world, and for letting me see how loving and warm a family can be.

Familly De Waal, for all the beautiful childhood moments I had and the wonderful holidays.

KHC Dragons, for being my club during my youth, where I fell in love with the game.

HC Bloemendaal, and all the people who contribute to the club, for creating the opportunity for me to play at a higher level, and the best competition, **Hoofdklasse,** in the world. Because of your beautiful club and people, I enjoy playing the game even more. It was a magnificent period.

The **President's Kid, Robby Novak,** who made the Peptalk and inspired me when I was young.

Jef Brouwers, for opening my mind and making me discover that success and reaching the top is about attitude and mentality. What happens on the inside impacts the outside.

Shane Mcleod, for being the right man at the right moment for our team, Red Lions, and for achieving the impossible for our country.

Michel Van den Heuvel, for all the work he has done, and for the time and energy he invested in the teams and people he works with. I love working with him. He really got the best out of me.

Adecco, for supporting and helping me follow my passion besides hockey. Because of their support, I can now educate myself more and follow my passion.

My **Sister, Sissi,** for who she is and how she helps the family and me, being there always. I love you. You are a queen. 'You came to me on an important moment and learned me to 'niet balen, maar stralen', 'don't worry, be happy'

My **brother, Sander,** who is the one who is bold and goes after his dreams as well. The brother's bond is a strong bond, and sometimes it gets challenged by the circumstances and events that life brings us. Let this bond be cherished and something to strive for, and let the challenges make it even stronger. Let love conquer always.

Ellen Schouppe, for getting me out of my dark hole after my setback in 2018, and for listening to me and understanding me when times were hard for me personally. Thank you for getting me back on track and making me come back stronger.

Delight yoga, where I can work on my inner strength and controlling my inner fire. Letting my mind free of thought helps me achieve more in my sports and in life.

Acknowledgements

Eric Verboom, who showed what passion for hockey really was, and who ignited my fire even more when I was young and talented; he really got the drive in me.

The Belgian Federation, for all the great work they are doing for the team and Belgian hockey.

Sport Vlaanderen, for helping athletes pursue their dreams and achieve the top.

Mark Lammers, for implementing the top sport culture with the Red Lions, and for pushing Belgian hockey.

Majid, my personal trainer. I met him when I couldn't do thirty push ups. He taught me how hard work and focus on your body can truly impact your level of physicality and mental strength, which impacted my game and my life—Beastmode.

Mick Beunen, for believing in me and pushing me to become better.

Red Lions, for inspiring me and challenging me to become a better hockey player. Your high standards made me raise mine. I thank you for being the good role model, and for inspiring me.

Rudi Mannaerts, for giving me spiritual guidance in times of physical exhaustion. You gave me spiritual inspiration.

Diederik Stockbroekx, for helping me in the times of injury, and the city Mol, and of course, Michiel Sleebus. A special journey was made during the World Cup when I got injured and got to know the beautiful people of Mol. Life has its ways, and it was a wonderful experience, one I will remember for the rest of my life.

Steven Stockbroekx, for helping me with the little projects I have.

Charly Janssens, my brother-in-law, for being the engineer of the family, making every clock tick faster. I can call him my brother for who he is and for how he loves my sister. Thank you for helping me with my top sport career, and for supporting me with your passion.

Jeroen Stockbroekx, for your continuous passion and support.

Osaka, my sponsor, who gave me my first sponsored stick, for creating a brand bigger than field hockey itself, transcending every other brand in the hockey world, and for inspiring me with your brand to become a better hockey player.

Lauranne Parmentier: you're crazy and weird. Like me!

Mom, the sacred feminine. You create life and you are love. Thank you for all the love you poured into me.

Les Brown, for giving me endless motivation and inspiration.

Raymond Aaron, for giving me inspiration while writing my book, and for transforming my life. With your energy, I was able to finish my book.

Chinmai, my book architect, who helped me write my book.

Gaur Gopal Das: reading your book during my setback of being injured, during the World Cup, inspired me and opened my mind on how to build up my life again from the inside.

Floris Geerts, for being the best field hockey commentator, and for expanding hockey through his voice and insights. You truly are a great commentator.

Karel Klaver, for being an awesome trainer, together with Michel.

Acknowledgements

Onze-Lieve-Vrouwecollege, for challenging me, knowing it wasn't always easy. Your high standards made me who I am today in the hockey world.

Examencommissie: because of your individual programs, I was able to finish my school, together with playing my top sport. You made it possible to combine the two.

Belfius, for being the main sponsor of the Red Lions, making it possible to inspire our country and the world, and for me to write this book.

Candriam, for believing in our team and for being one of our main sponsors, making it possible for our team to follow our passion and be inspired.

Tom Mertens: We have been through a lot together, which makes our connection strong. Thanks for helping me come back stronger every time.

Han Stagefright, for overcoming your fear of stage and giving me a free lunch! And **Envita Hasler** as well. Postulating all the way.

Emma Aaron, for inspiring me with your book #success.

Lewis Howes, for giving me daily inspiration in the car, on my way to **HC Bloemendaal and The Red Lions,** with your podcast and your story. Going from a broke athlete to a successful entrepreneur inspires me greatly.

Ed Mylett, for teaching me to *max out* my life.

Andrew Lamont, for teaching me that in life you have to be grateful for what you have.

Frederique Constant, for making beautiful watches, and inspiring people to follow their passion.

Tesla, for following your vision and pushing through, even though everyone is against you.

4ocean, for cleaning the ocean! And for taking responsibility to make our planet cleaner.

Radio 1, MNM, VTM and VRT, for inviting us regularly, and for presenting our story in a good way.

Het Vriendenhuis and Thomas: You are a gift. A miracle. You make me smile every time.

Oprah: you are truly inspiring.

Martin Klipp, for teaching me spirituality.

Michel Senior Deville, for joining my workshop and bringing me in contact with **Erwin Van Denberg.**

Govert and Maarten, for helping me to find myself, besides in hockey.

Boyan, for having the guts to go after your dream to clean the ocean, and for following your vision and being a role model for every young aspiring person.

Philippe Goldberg, for inspiring me to become a hockey player.

Lars, for helping me with my revalidation.

And, of course, every member of the national team, or former member of the Red Lions, for becoming better men.

Anyone else I didn't mention, friends or family... thank you for being in my life and making it awesome!

And if you want the thing bad enough,
to go out and fight for it
To work day and night for it
To give up your time, your peace, and your sleep for it
If all that you dream and scheme is about it
And life seems useless and worthless without it
And if you gladly sweat for it and fret for it and plan for it
And lose all your terror of the opposition for it
And if you simply go after that thing that you want
With all of your capacity, strength, and sagacity
Faith, hope, and confidence and stern pertinacity
If neither cold, poverty, famine, nor gout
Sickness nor pain, of body and brain,
Can keep you away from the thing that you want
If dogged and grim you beseech and beset it,
With the help of God you will get it

If an egg is
broken from an outside force,
life ends.

If broken from an **inside force**,
life **begins**.

Great things
start inside.

Chapter Eternity

Be Intentional

The best time is now
I am the greatest
I believe in myself
Today is better than yesterday
This training is the best training ever
This speech is the best speech ever
This book will be the best book ever
I speak from the heart
I am kind
I am unstoppable
I have drive
And passion !
I inspire
I help others
I have peace of mind
I am financially stable
I have great relationships
I feel good about myself
I smile
I am grateful every day
I leave a positive legacy
I am world class
I am the captain of my fate and the master of my soul

I am love
I live daily
I love
I spread positivity
I achieve my dreams and goals
I grow
I learn
I serve
I pray
I reflect

The best time is
NOW

Intention

Intention is something that has caught my interest. In sports, your intent could be hundreds of things. You can go play golf with your friends just for fun. But maybe, after a while, you'll want to win the thing, or you want to improve your hitting. So, unconsciously, your intent can change, and suddenly you are cursing and throwing your club in the woods. You can play hockey as a way to relax yourself after a hard day at work. Or go to the gym to blow off some steam. But you can also aim to win the thing. To be the best you possibly can. As your intent is chosen, you'll find yourself attracted to the thing you are aiming at.

As I prepare myself for the World Cup, it is very natural for me to train every day—to start eating healthy, to change my habits, to go to bed early, to rise early—to give it all I've got. My intent is to be the best I possibly can. So I'll look for things that support that intent. Smoking is bad. That's a fact, so I don't smoke. Drinking is bad. That's a fact, so I don't drink. If I see people drinking and smoking or eating fast food, I'll notice that they have different intents. They will not be going to the Olympics any time soon. That self destructive behaviour is something interesting. They are off track of where they want to be.

As you become conscious of your intent, you'll start to see it and act towards it. If my mind can conceive it, and my heart can believe it, then I can achieve it. When you are in class, visualize your intent. Is it to be the greatest student that ever lived? Or is it to laugh with your classmates? Is it to annoy the teacher? When you start with your intent, you ready yourself to become the person to fulfil that intent.

Grow

First of all, I was at the three-day, *get your book done,* boot camp of Raymond. And the most amazing thing happened. I get excited when these things happen. On the first day, I was writing, and I already had my chapters done. We were in a big room with about 30 other upcoming authors, and I was sitting next to Florence. Florence was this beautiful black woman. At the end of the three days, she smiled at me and said she wanted to meet my mother, because then she could say to her that she was adopting me.

One of the assignments of the 10-10-10 program is that you have to write your ten chapters down before you begin the actual writing of your book. Like most of us, when we have an idea about writing a book, we just begin writing, without any structure or plan. The chapters give you a clear structure and plan. But then I came up with a new idea for a chapter—a new chapter— together with my new friend, Florence. It was my eleventh chapter, because I already had ten. When we needed to read our chapters to each other, I picked my neighbour, Florence. And as I came to my eleventh chapter and read it to Florence— "Chapter 11, Intention, with bullet points: Grow, Help, Contribute, Love, Have Fun"—she looked at me with her beautiful smile, and said, with a sparkle in her eye: "That should be your first chapter." And I started laughing because she was telling me what to do.

The next day, Raymond gave a short lesson about the spiritual and the physical universe. The physical universe is the result of the spiritual universe. Thoughts become things. Like a business plan. You brainstorm together. It becomes a plan. Then you execute the plan. Then, of course, you see how difficult it can become in the physical world to implement your ideas and thoughts. In sport, you would say you begin with a dream. "Teamwork makes the dream work; coming together is a beginning; staying together is progress; working together is success." Intentions become your reality. You understand what *hot* is when you understand what *not hot* is… Or cold.

Postulates are thoughts. I wanted to be an athlete when I was young. Then, suddenly, my world started to give me ways to become one. I was selected for the national team, and suddenly I found myself surrounded by top athletes and weight rooms. Funny how the universe helps you in achieving your dreams and ideas. Only when you are fully awake and see the opportunities you are constantly given, you can fully emerge yourself in it. It's because Raymond wants to get people to write books that I'm now writing my own book, and because of his program. Also because I want to write one, and some voice in my head is pushing me to write it.

Hopefully, writing this book makes people understand more what it is that we, as fulltime athletes, are going through. Also, this book can give me the strength and the opportunity to continue doing what I love. So, we found each other because, somewhere in the world, one man had an idea that meets the need of someone else (me) somewhere else in the world. Isn't that magical? People would say that's just a coincidence, or that I'm lucky I get support—all those not-so-fun terms—instead of thinking the things that are happening are spiritual phenomena, which makes the world a better place.

The last part of his small presentation, he actually didn't want to do in the beginning. He didn't want to do it because most of us, when we sit and listen to someone, are just like cows in a field. If you would just look at your own face, once in your life, when you are listening to someone, it would open your eyes. You would just see a boring facial expression. Of course, it also depends on how the message is presented. But sometimes you can have an impact on that as well, if you look alive and interested in what is about to happen, or ask questions. But Raymond was willing to give a small explanation about intentions: Some things come from, as some people would say, the spiritual world. They just come up. They have no beginning and no end. Suddenly, the idea or intention is there, and when you give attention to them, they seem to grow and give you a lot of energy. And then, afterwards, I explained that I just made that one my first chapter. So, actually, what he explained about the physical and spiritual world—the intentions, postulates, etc.—actually just happened to me. My heart began to pound a little harder, and I felt that the universe was guiding me, which felt really powerful.

Growing hurts. When I was young, about 16, I was this small but tall guy, and people would call me *asperge*. I didn't fit in a medium or in a small. So everything I wore was either too short or too long. I had a baby face. The older, *cool* guys laughed at me, and called me Pimples, etc. It's like that as well when you want to achieve a dream, a vision, a business, or writing a book. When you start where you are, it looks like it is miles away from what you want it to be. Like when you want to look like that model with those jeans and shirt (large), with all the girls around him, but you have a baby face with pimples. It hurts. You need to have patience. You may not get everything, but some things, like the pimples, will go away.

You can find help, like how writing a book through Raymond and his online book program, 10/10/10, helped me; or by studying, or getting to know yourself better and knowing others better. Be interested in others. And when you have the growth mindset, things get very easy. When you accept that you don't know everything, and that you are willing to learn and to grow, and go beyond everything you've ever done, you have to grow, to better your personal best. Life becomes fantastic. And when you fail, like I did often along the way, you get back up! Because *"every setback is a setup for a comeback."* – Les Brown. When you have that mindset, where you just keep coming back, day in and day out because you know you can grow your mind, your body, and your spirit, you can be limitless!

The first time I started going to the gym, I couldn't do fifty pushups. Now I can do 100 pushups. But I found help. Majid, my personal trainer, helped me take the first steps. I wasn't selected for the national team, and I didn't go to regular school anymore. This is where I learned to push through the pain. And I went through pain, and I had to stretch and push myself. But when you then feel you can go further, it's beautiful. This is where your body and your mind can adapt and grow through the pain. It's like a quantum leap. I remember feeling tired and broken every day during the preparation for the Olympics. But when the trainings were finally over, and we just had to play the games, I felt

I was flying over the pitch. I felt light but powerful; calm but determined.

The same is with the mind. I remember going for a walk in the park, and it opened up my brain. It felt like a breeze went through it. And when I meditate with Headspace, I feel my mind growing, or literally feel my head spacing out (without using any substances here). When I read the book, *"Power of Positive Thinking,"* by Norman Vincent Peale, my mind grew in new ways and changed the game.

When you are open to growing, you'll take on challenges with a certain optimism, like a sprinter who jumps over the hurdles with ease. You'll feel the fear but do it anyhow, because you know that you can grow. And you are supported, just like my little nephew Jack. He's one and a half years old, and he just learned to walk, but he fell over a thousand times. Each time, he got back up. It's the same in life. You fall. You learn. You get back up, and you walk a little further. Even if you crawl, you keep moving forward, until you end up running a marathon or running for your country at the Olympics. You never know when the universe will call on you to fulfil your destiny. You'd better be ready.

Serve

Provide more service than you get paid for.

A year before the Rio Olympics in 2016, we had a breakdown with our team. We didn't achieve our goal, and that was reaching the final of the European Championships in London. We failed big time by losing against Germany, 4–0; winning against France with just 3–2; and drawing against Ireland. This came down to going back home as favorites, not fulfilling, once again, our potential. It was very frustrating. Our coach left, and we were in the dark as a team and as players. Again, this was ten months before the Olympics. Then came Shane McLeod, a *Kiwi* from New Zealand. He coached some of the Brussels guys at Waterloo Ducks Hockey Club, so we had an idea of who he was. I respected him because you could always feel his presence, and he coached the Ducks during some of their best years, as well as the Waterloo women's team. He had ten months to get us at the podium in Rio, something that never happened before for Belgium. One of the things that stood out for me was that he asked the group to come up with ideas to help the team.

Sometimes you feel a new groove in your brain when someone says something, and it just opens up a whole new world. So I had an idea somewhere in the back of my mind to make smoothies for the team during lunch breaks. This is something I thought would be helpful because the food wasn't always that great, and smoothies can be very nutritious, especially when you already have to drink shakes every day and eat three or four times a day. A smoothie can be refreshing and healthy, and it can make you really happy and ease your spirit a bit when you're in a high pressure environment. I had to buy the fruit, etc., buy a blender, make the smoothie, and give it to everyone. After training, I would run to the kitchen to make them so everyone could have them during their dinner every day. Of course, there were some days I was so wrecked from training that I skipped one. But in the long term, you could say I was pretty consistent with my idea. And it was about serving my teammates out of love. It meant that I had to serve a smoothie to the player that was my opponent on the field a minute ago during a trainings game.

Sometimes I would be really frustrated about my level, or because I lost some duels and 1v1. But then, making the smoothie eased my mind again, and actually gave me energy! While others were done after the training, craving their couch, I was reborn and ready! There was something about the service for others that gave me even more energy. I called it the smoothie effect. Also, seeing the happy faces of staff members and team members, after I had given them my smoothie, made me happy, which again, gave me enormous amounts of energy. Guys were even saying they were making the smoothies themselves at home in the morning.

As a defender, you also have to put yourself back for others to thrive. You are defending the castle whilst others are approaching the goal. But when players in the team are starting to serve and play, not only for themselves but also to see the benefit for serving others, there you get into a different area. Life can be good in that place. And it starts with training, every day. For me, it started with the smoothies.

Love

What if, every day, you get up with the intention of love? What happens? Every challenge that comes your way, you take it on, out of love—out of love for your brothers, your sisters, your parents, people who helped you—for everyone. What if you love everyone, even if they hurt you? You answer with love. I know that can seem a little out of the ordinary. Every day, you see hate, violence, death, war, addiction, and broken hearts… What does it take for a heart to overflow with love, even for those whom you have the hardest time loving, or even thinking about sending them a text? Maybe those are the ones who need it the most.

On the playing field, whether it is at work or on a hockey pitch, you come across tiny little challenges. Some people ignore them; others don't see them; others see them and take on the challenge—things that challenge your love for your teammates. I like to say those are my brothers whom I fight for. And then you can say, "Yeah, but what did they do for you, for you to say they are your brothers?" That's where I believe that every good thing has to start with you. If you wait until someone else has to do it before you do, then life can be very challenging and boring.

Smile first, and then see what will happen. Do you love your brothers so much that you can forgive them after they have made a mistake or made the same wrong decision again? Do you love your teammate when he doesn't follow up what was said in the team meeting? Do you love your teammate when he doesn't show up fresh and energized to do the work that needs to be done? Do you love him so much that you are ready to give him your precious love and energy to lift him up? Do you love your teammate so much that you give him a smoothie after training, when actually, maybe, he doesn't deserve your love and attention, because he is thinking only of himself and not the others? Or maybe he's not training well, training at a different level, or talking behind other people's backs. He's only serving his purpose. Or do you let bitterness, hatred, and thinking less of others, take over? Can you let go? Can you see that everyone is doing their best, in their way, and in the way that they think is best for them? Hurt people, hurt other people. Love can hurt. It will hurt. But you must overcome any challenges that make love difficult. Often, the people you hate the most are the ones who need your love the most. I was a man of hate and despair who opened his heart for love and hope. As the sun follows the sun, you must follow love.

This morning, I had to get up at 7:30. Yesterday, I followed a zoom class of Raymond's, with twenty other people who all share their goals, dreams, and challenges they need to overcome. I thought, why not? It would be good fun. After the zoom class, which is an online mentoring class where everyone shares their wins and goals of the past month, Raymond gives his tips on how to achieve more of them or achieve them in a better way. In the end, my father, mother, brother, and sister were also listening. They were curious about what this Raymond was all about. And they loved it. It was pretty awesome because you follow an online class with people from London, Toronto, and Belgium. You can see all the faces, and the one who speaks gets the full screen. Raymond leads the class. Everyone is a bit shy because we're all new. But it opened my world.

After the zoom class, my brother wanted to present his presentation that he had to give for the investors. Of course, he was excited. He's developing a digital platform for the diplomat tax free market. Diplomats now have to fill in lots of paperwork, as do the government institutions, to reclaim and refund the tax of goods. This whole process is being digitalized, and it is a big project. The idea came from my father. He has been working on it already for ten years. I gave my brother some tips I learned from giving presentations, like finding your anchor moment. Excitement can become stress. And when the fun stops, the stress starts. Suddenly, you start seeing everything falling apart, and that is when, actually, everything does fall apart.

Finding an anchor moment and tapping into that energy can be really helpful. You have to sit calmly, with your hands on your knees. Think about a moment in your life where you felt really good, in control, happy, fulfilled, and excited. Breathe in, losing the verbal fossils, like "ahems" and "so's." Before we went to bed, I asked him if he wanted to know what I usually say to myself before I go on stage or have a speaking event before hundreds of people: I say, "You deserve to be here, and you did everything you possibly can. Now get it done." Then, he said, "It's not the first time I'm doing this." And there, he had me— thinking I knew it all. For me, it helped, but maybe it doesn't for someone else. Ah, well. I said what I thought I had to say. It's up to him if he wants to use it.

Knowledge is power—wrong. Knowledge that you *use* is power. Have you ever seen someone doing something that wasn't in the best interest of the team? It may have been in *his* best interest. And to be honest, everyone needs a healthy focus on self-interest. In order to help other people or to be happy, you, yourself, need to be happy. On the other hand, when your self-interest is at the cost of someone else, it is something to think about. Enlightened self-interest is where you go for what is yours in the universe, but in a way that you, yourself, win, and the others around you win as well. That's the right way to do it. So, when you see someone close to you do something that isn't in the best interest of his neighbour, teammate, or family, what should you do? You see someone addicted to drugs, which impacts his relationships in a bad way. He is not going for his dreams and goals because of fear, and he is slowly sliding away into the abyss. Well, there is knowledge you have, which you are not using, to make an adjustment. Moments like these are always around us: tiny little decisions we make to not use our knowledge or better judgment; being silent and not expressing your feelings—knowledge isn't power if you are not using it. Decisions, not conditions, determine my destiny.

Look at your life and recall some decisions you made based on conditions and not on what you wanted or desired. You were unhappy and lonely, so you decided to have a relationship with someone you didn't really like. You didn't have enough money, so that business seemed impossible. It was raining, so you didn't go do that workout. Your country had an economic crisis, so you waited for the government to help you. You didn't like the teacher, so you let your grades go down because of it. Those decisions to stay in your bed, to not go to work, to not study, to not write that book, may push your dreams away for a whole six months or a whole year, or even for a whole lifetime—just because you didn't go for it that one day! Its starts now, with you, at this moment.

Things happen for you, not to you. There are 86,400 seconds in a day. Every minute is a window of opportunity to do what you would like to do to achieve your goals and dreams, or to learn something new. Every second is precious. Some choices will lead to failures from which you must learn. Some choices will turn out to be mistakes. Some will make you win. Some will turn out to be the best decisions you've ever made. But most of us waste our precious time by having bad habits (e.g., watching TV and eating Cheetos).

The time between our birth and death is a present given to us. Often, we waste this precious time by seeking small pleasures, avoiding minor discomforts, and pursuing trivial goals. You tend to do the easy things, and your life will seem hard. When you do the hard things, life will be easy. There is an app, *Moment*, which clocks the time that you are looking at your phone. There are days that I'm looking at my phone for three hours. That's huge. Of course, I often listen to podcasts and inspiring, motivational videos. Or I put on Waze in the car.

We are also too easily offended, and too consumed with the opinion of others. Somebody could say something, and it could wander in our minds for days, poisoning our minds. If we are not careful, we simply begin to exist and not really live. The average lifespan of a person is 78 years. Of those years, twenty-eight will be spent sleeping, and seven of those sleeping years are spent lying awake at night with worry. Factor in the average eleven years watching television or surfing on the internet, ten and a half years working, four years driving, the years spent eating, getting dressed, and doing mundane tasks, and it leaves approximately *eight years to live your life.* Now that you know this, how deep would your gratitude for each and every precious moment in your life become? What would this do to your sense of urgency to achieve what you want? To go for your goals and your dreams?

The top five biggest regrets of dying people are: "I wish I'd had the courage to live a life true to myself, not the life others expected of me;" "I wish I hadn't worked so hard;" "I wish I'd had the courage to express my feelings;" "I wish I had stayed in touch with my friends;" "I wish that I had let myself be happier." When you truly learn these things—read it slowly, and read it again and again—and *act* upon it, your life will change.

The reason I wrote this book is because I now had some success in my life, and I want to make it clear that it is not just me. I play on two world class teams. I have a wonderful family. I am surrounded by world-class players and people. I have professional staff who have supported me through the years.

They made me better. I learned to be disciplined. I learned that the way I think, live, believe, and speak, all impacts the people around me and, therefore, on a team, influences the results and the performance of the team. Therefore, out of respect for the people around me, it is my duty to be the best version of myself, to lift the people around me up, and take personal responsibility for my level, my life, and my development.

You become like the 5 people you spend the most time with. And therefore, what I am, and the success I have, is because of the people I am around. Therefore, I am grateful every day that I can be around these people and teams. Some will say that I'm just on these teams that all play on a low level. Why bother to show my best self? This is not worth it. Well, start small. When you set out to be disciplined—to be passionate; to be driven; to be humble and smart; to do the best you possibly can—when you start with the people you have and where you are, someday you may well end up doing those same things on a much larger scale. When you can't find ways to find a job or something you like, start at your home with your family. Try and be valuable for them. Help in the kitchen. Help with the garden. Know that in order to get something out of life, you must first start giving. And with giving, the process of receiving will start.

Imagine that there is a castle with all the resources you wish to have, and to go into that castle, you have to knock at a door. The door is opened by the doorkeeper. What question would you ask him or her? A lot of people would say, "Give me money. If I could just have the money, then I would be successful." Sadly, this is not the way to go. Ask, "How can I earn this money? What do I have to do in order to be valuable and be deserving of this money?" You don't get what you want; you get what you deserve. You don't go to the ground and yell, "Give me my potatoes! Give me flowers and trees!" If that soil could speak, it would say, "You fool! If you want all this, then bring me seeds." What you reap is what you sow.

I want to help a lot of people through this book. I know it is my illusion. But serving others is something that gives me energy. It gives me meaning and purpose. That's why I like playing this game. It inspires and serves people. Also, chasing your dream gives others permission to follow theirs. Often, you think that the ideas you have, and the dreams or goals you have, are to be kept secret so that you can take the fruit of those ideas. You think about yourself first, and only when you have your comfort, you will give to others. As it says in Luke, Chapter 6, Verse 38, *"Give, and it will be given to you."* And, as in Galatians, Chapter 6, Verse 7, *"Whatever a person sows, this he will also reap."* This is the same with faith. When you expect to fail, you will fail. When you expect to win, you shall win. But then, you say, "I expected to win yesterday, but I lost the game. And I expected to succeed on my exam, but I failed that too."

I ask you to broaden your scope. When you expect to win, your body, mind, and soul will look to get that into your life. You will attract things that will help you to win. And even when you fail once, you'll go again the next day. When you fail, it is only a test for you to see how truly you believe to win. How deep are you willing to go? When you give up after the first loss or failure, you didn't really, in your core, expect to win. And even then, when you have given it your all, and when there is nothing left that you could do, and when you are standing there on the stage or in your business, you can say to yourself, "I have done everything in my power," and you could still fail or lose. Even then, you are winning. People will respect you. They will applaud you.

One example was the US Open final between Del Potro and Djokovic—two titans fighting each other, suffering for victory, with great sportsmanship. After three sets, Djokovic was set to be the champion. The stadium was packed with 24,000 people, people with all kind of status—actors, politicians, artists—the finest people. When Del Potro lost the final, even Djokovic showed his respect. The people were applauding, because they knew Del Potro gave it his all. He fought well. He pushed his limits. In order to get to the level he was playing at, he had to become the best version of himself. And that is the greatest victory of all—when even when you lose, you inspire others to be great. So, even when you lose, you still win. Del Potro is currently number four in the world.

When I was little, we would always go to Holland, to the sea, for holidays. We had a holiday house and would chill out with our family, and enjoy the sun, the sea, and the French fries with sate sauce and mayonnaise. It was the only place where we could watch television because, in Belgium, in our home, my parents threw the television out. We would still be able to watch movies. The movie nights were always on the weekend. We would then go to the movie center and rent the movies. It's funny because we always forgot to take them back, and we had to pay big fines to the movie center. They would see us coming and say, "Oh, no." Because we couldn't watch any television during the week, on the weekend, we went full loco with the movies. Just to watch a movie together with the family is something wonderful.

So, back to the summer. As I was watching television, the Summer Olympics was on. I don't really remember what year it was, but I can clearly remember wondering and asking my father why Belgium had such a small delegation, and not even a good team in the delegation. There wasn't one good performing team. Not one. And now I know how hard it is, and why that is.

But every time it's hard now, or I want to quit or throw in the towel, I think about that little boy who was looking at the television and dreaming. And I say to myself, "I'm doing this for you, my friend, so you can dream on...."

One other aspect I started noticing now is that when I found my purpose and could see it clearly, I started seeing it everywhere. The average person has 75,000 thoughts every day, and 91% are exactly the same as the day before. It isn't hard to see why some people stay in the exact same spot in life as it relates to career, sport, fitness, finance, etc. Do you ever think about what you think about? Thoughts are like magnets; they draw to you that which you think about regularly. They also create the filter you see the world through. If you want real change, you must first change what you are thinking about. Change just 10% of your thoughts, and you can dramatically change your life. It is powerful and, most important of all, *under your control!"* You have a mental filter that can work with you or against you. *Pay close attention to this topic because it is the most important part of my success.*

There is a bundle of nerves at our brainstem, called the Reticular Activating System (RAS), which acts as a gatekeeper, filtering out irrelevant information and allowing only relevant information to enter our awareness. This little bit of brain matter is responsible for filtering out the massive amounts of information that your body, and the world around it, is constantly throwing its way. It filters out all the things that would prove our beliefs false, and instead, works overtime on filtering in all the things that will prove our beliefs to be true. Your RAS takes what you focus on and creates a filter for it. It then sifts through the data and presents only the pieces that are important to you. All this happens without you noticing it, of course. The RAS programs itself to work in your favour without you actively doing anything. That is powerful, isn't it? Now that

I'm in a good functioning team, I can see bad functioning teams everywhere. Or bad relationships. It's because my focus is creating the best team, and being the best team player possible.

When you believe you're going to grow a big successful business, or have a great income, the RAS starts working to filter in all the experiences that will prove this to be your reality. Specifically, if you believe people need what you have, the RAS will begin to reveal opportunities that may have always been there but are now highlighted as a result of your focus. This focus causes them to be relevant to you. Sadly, most people among us don't know how to use the RAS in a positive way. They only see problems and worries, and therefore attract even more problems and worries into their lives. The worst part is that they blame other people for it; usually people that are successful and attracting good things into their lives. They think that it is because of them being successful that they are not. That's what some people call *the haters*. Haters love to hate.

Break this cycle by focusing and obsessing on what you want, and not on what you don't want. Anything you want in life requires your total obsession. *Your obsessions become your possessions.* Understand that the RAS doesn't attract the things you need. It's not by focussing on a house that you will get a house suddenly. Everything you need has always been there. You just didn't see them because they were not deemed significant at the time. Once you focus on a goal, your obsession and RAS are heightened, and you filter in all the elements that support your goal. You literally begin to see, hear, and feel things that always existed, but you never noticed before. The RAS is the greatest tool and magnet for success in the world. It is a God-given survival tool that we all possess but rarely utilize.

A lot of businesses or start-ups struggle with the basics of good team performance. They hire someone who isn't committed to the project—who asks when he or she can go home; who isn't prepared to do the overtime, or to go the extra mile to make the company successful; who sits around scrolling on the internet, looking for the next meme or stupid video about someone drinking beer out of a shoe. Going out that one night or sleeping through that one morning can push your dream away for years. It's all in your control. You are more powerful than you can ever begin to imagine.

Exercise

(Your *because* becomes your *I want to*)
My example:
I want to *play hockey*
Because *I love playing hockey and want to reach the top.*

I want to *do stuff I love and reach for the top*
Because *that makes me happy and inspires others.*

I want to *be happy and inspire others*
Because *then I can make others happy and inspire myself (as in, "wow, look what you are doing!").*

I want to *make others happy and inspire myself and others*
Because *I believe the world needs happiness and inspiration!*

YOUR TURN

I want to ….
Because ….

I want to ….
Because ….

I want to ….
Because ….

I want to ….
Because ….

I want to ….
Because ….

Do YOGA. But be LOVE, always.

Meditate every day. Do yoga. Get yourself in uncomfortable positions, positions where you feel the stretch. Your breath is challenged. You need focus. You train your focus, and when you train your focus in one area, you feel it in every other area of your life. Focus on your breath, your inner flame. Make it grow. Make it as big as the Olympic flame. Be passionate. Be lively. Don't stop when you feel uncomfortable. That's when you grow. Continue. And do it at least four times a week if you want to feel the magic quickly.

Chapter 2

Postulates

Feeling Like a Failure

At school, they always said to me, "If you want it, Emmanuël, you can do it." Every time, I didn't really understand what they meant. I was just having fun— playing with my friends, trying to get the attention of the prettiest girl in the classroom, annoying the teacher sometimes with my behaviour—just to see how far I could go. It ended up with my agenda full of notes, visiting the principal every week… several times. And then the grades were terrible. I don't really remember if they were always bad, but I remember that there was always a point where I was absolutely disorganised.

Of course, I had good moments where life was easy and everything went good. But then there were those intense moments in my life where life just seemed turbulent, and things would happen. I would have to ask my classmates for notes, and ask them questions about what to learn and what not to learn. Now I realise I must have been a pain in the ass for them, because they did all the hard work during the year, and then this guy would show up: me. But they always told me that my potential was really big. They were often disappointed in my behaviour and attitude. When the bad grades would show up, I would be very motivated and eager to start over and do everything the right way: take notes, concentrate better in class, do my homework properly.

And sure, there were times when I would be very diligent, and then the grades would follow. And then the teachers said: "You see, Emmanuël!"

I think the trouble was that I lost focus along the way. I lost focus on what I wanted. Or the short-term goals took over the long-term goals. The monkey-mind took over. Also, I always had ideas and things to do. I remember that my brother and I (who is three years older) were studying upstairs in our room on a warm summer night, with the windows open. I would yell: "Sander, in for a quick ping pong break?!" Then, he would say, "Of course." We would come back, three hours later, covered in sweat and dirt from diving and putting everything we had into the ping pong court, feeling like world-class ping pong masters. You never know if, one day, one of us would end up at the ping pong Olympics. You just never know... or at the Olympics doing any other sport.

Anyhow, going back to study was hard; so hard, it felt like my soul was dying. That was what happened in crucial moments during my schooldays. And then, hockey came onto my path. I was selected for the national programs, which would, step-by-step, take over my whole world. But I was going to school in the Onze-Lieve-vrouwecollege. And when I do something, I always want to shoot to the top. It's just in my nature. I like doing it. So, I would have to choose between hockey and school, at one point, doing Latin and math. Now I can understand why it felt so hard. I was pulled into two different universes.

The combination started to get lethal. I would be tired on the school banks from Sunday's game, and then get more tired from the trainings in the evening. I would come home and procrastinate on my homework because I wanted to hear the stories of my family. We could just sit around the dinner table and talk for hours and hours. We would sit at the dining table. We are the type of family where no stone is left unturned. Everything is on the table, no matter what it is. *That's* just amazing. I love my family. I remember talking about life and experiences, and it was something I loved doing.

Feeling Pressure

But then, as much as I was having fun with meeting new people, learning, etc., there was always this pressure. Suddenly, you would have to start studying for the exams. And the easy subjects would go fine. But the subjects, like math and Latin, were the type of subjects where you couldn't start to learn them just the night before and then improvise and go on your feeling. These subjects took hard work and focus throughout the year and in the classes, something I had trouble with. I realised this several times during the exam period. Like, shit, I did it again! I was totally unprepared. It's not that I didn't like doing these subjects... It's just because of all of my interests and hobbies and friends; I couldn't do them properly and profoundly with the right attitude and diligence. I just wanted too much.

And now I had to call my niece to get the copies of the Latin texts, and I had to ask which parts of the subject were important. And oh, it was horrible; especially when people would say to me, "Emmanuël, you are so smart, and when you do your best, you can do it!" But I didn't know how!! It was terrible; I always managed to screw up. It ended up as a fact that whatever I did, people would say: "You have talent; you could go far in this." So, the pressure built. Whenever I didn't do anything at a high level, I would feel miserable, and so terrible. Plus, the fact I have a perfectionist mind makes it even harder for me to let something go.

Choosing is losing, I thought. The hockey story became bigger and bigger. At one point, I stopped the national U16 team. My grades were not what they should be, and my parents and I decided that it would be better for me to focus on my studies more so that my grades would go up. So, school was my number one priority. But it just didn't work. It was hard for me: my grades didn't go up; motivation dropped little by little; and I had trouble getting in line. Then, the national hockey team called me again to ask if I would like to start trainings again. And I said yes to preparation for the U18 European cup. We became European champions with our team. In a pool game against Spain, I saved a ball from the line, twice in a row. It gave me a great feeling to be important to my team, and to make my family proud and happy. From that point on, you are part of a *golden generation*, and people would refer to this generation as having great potential.

We would win the European Championships U21 a year later, with almost the same group. We started believing we could beat anyone. The self- confidence was high. I would quickly be selected for the first team of my club at a young age. So, also there, the pressure was rising, not only at school but also at hockey. The thing is that I would be able to sometimes deliver great results, and get amazing grades, have lots of friends, be very happy, and do good at school; and then, somehow, there were times where I didn't manage to meet the expectations, at a different point in life.

A Snail Who Wants to Become a Lion

During the European Cup in Amsterdam, I was running with Julien Rysman, our physiotherapist, in the forest. I was injured and would join the team in the third pool game against Spain. As we were running, we bumped into some snails. And as I thought about these snails, I started thinking like a snail. We were running and moving fast, from one point to the other, while the snail has to do the same distance with much more effort, and it takes a lot longer for the snail to catch up. Julien and I run easily what, for the snail, must be an enormous endeavour.

As we ran up the hill, just like that, the snail must have looked at that hill, and thought, "What if I could go up that hill?" He would have to consider his mission of going up the hill, with his colleague snails. He would have to think how and why, because going up that hill would take a lifetime. It would mean giving up his snail house, leaving everything behind, making the sacrifices, and leaving his snail family behind to reach the top. He would bump into predators, and encounter fallen trees and rotting leaves. Is he willing to leave the well-known path, to attain his dream and follow his heart, knowing that it might mean the end of his life? Will he be able to tell the tale, or like many other snails, never come back? Imagine the snail and what must be going through his mind. Meanwhile, the ground is shaking because of two giants running by. That snail has a dream of one day becoming the lion of his pack. He has dreams. He somehow feels that his slime will glide him to the top. He is willing to abandon everything he knows to attain that goal—that dream life—slowly but steadily.

Your PROBLEM is your GIFT.

Your problem is your gift. Your problem is that you think you shouldn't have any. Every problem is a present you need to unpack. Lots of times, you encounter a problem. And we live in that problem for a long time, not realising it is exactly what we need to grow. Often, confronting a problem is hurtful. It's not nice. So, we avoid it. But it sometimes takes one conversation with someone who can help you, or who went through the same problem. It is that one brief moment where someone asks you if everything is alright, and you are afraid to tell them that there are actually a lot of things that are not alright. It's looking in the mirror, and you taking full responsibility of your life. Be hungry to solve the problems you face when no one believes in you, and when everyone says that it isn't possible. But know that others can help you. That's where the opportunities lie. And solving your own problem can help you help people who face the same problem. Life is great.

Children don't learn from people they don't like!

Going for a Dream

In the summer, we always go to our summer bungalow in Holland. We go sailing there and chill out, doing typical summer things. Also, we could watch television there. I loved it. In Belgium, at home, we didn't have any TV. Our parents thought it wasn't good. They would tell us to go outside and play. Also, we would be very addicted. I could watch TV for hours and hours. Anyhow, as I was saying, I was watching TV during summer, and then this show would come on about the Olympics. It was a summer when the Olympics took place. So now I could watch all these different athletes and teams going for their dreams of winning at the Olympics. "Wow!" I would say. "Isn't that amazing?" I would watch and dream of myself being there. These people all looked so happy and amazing, and it gave me a great feeling about life. Then I would see Belgium. And I would wonder why there weren't any teams. There wasn't even one successful team. I remember I was really curious about why other countries had these successful teams working as one, but Belgium just didn't have any.

This was when I was really young, and when hockey and school problems were far away. When I was eighteen, I decided to leave school. I had to do the fifth grade over again. I decided I didn't wanted to do that and left school. I thought that things would turn out as they always do, and that I would figure a way out. A lot of my friends from my generation also dropped out of my school. It was something that happened more and more at that time. Also, there were critics that said that schools, in general, were stuck in the past, and missed implementing modern technologies in the school. So, it wasn't weird to quit school. Other guys were doing it as well.

I quit school, but it was with the plan to focus fully on hockey and finish my school through an individual learning plan. You would have to sign up for exams, and the rest you had to do for yourself. I realised then that school wasn't so bad. Doing everything by yourself is a very big wakeup call. It puts a mirror in front of you where you see all your flaws. You can't blame anyone else anymore. You can't blame the teachers for being lousy teachers. You can't blame students in the class for distracting you. It's just you and yourself battling, suffering, and being alone. And then, there was the hockey field—my other battlefield—where I would start dreaming of getting on the national team. I decided that in order to become a better player, I would have to go to a personal trainer to get my body strong. It also helped my mental aspect. He would push me through pain to get me to places I had never been before.

Sacrifices

My life changed drastically from being at school—having a girlfriend there, having made friends—and I disappeared. I chose a totally different life without really realising it. I chose a different path. I remember being really down sometimes, not knowing if this was the right thing. I felt really shitty at some points, with feelings I couldn't really describe. I felt a bit lost. But when I was on that hockey pitch, I would feel good—at least sometimes. There were also other times where it was also shitty. I realised that no matter what path you take, everybody ends up with a certain amount of bad feelings, failures, heartbreaks, doubts, disbelief, etc.... And there is always that one person you end up confronting: yourself. That guy, with his flaws, stands around the corner, reminding you of all your failures and doubts, whispering in your ear. But then I would listen to YouTube videos from Kid President...

"Two roads diverged in the woods, and I took the road less travelled. And it hurt man! Really bad! Rocks! Thorns! And glass! Not cool, Robert Frost!"

As I took a different path than most of my friends, I lost most of them (Not lost them, but you know, you lose contact.). I couldn't attend the usual social events. I had a different schedule. A lot of them didn't understand why I would not come to parties and would not drink alcohol. They would laugh: "Is it for that hockey game??" A lot of them didn't understand what I was feeling. Little did they know that five years later, we would win the silver Olympic medal. It sure wasn't an easy process, but it was worth it! Other sacrifices were that I would be tired all the time, and hungry; I would eat like a horse. Your body is constantly in recovery mode, clearing all the toxic stuff from your body, which you create during trainings.

You lose friends, and you lose your social life. You lose the opportunity to go on the school trip at the end of your last year at school with all your classmates. I was missing the student life; missing all the parties; missing all the gossip; missing everything a normal kid of my age would be doing—all for a dream, and all because, somehow, it feels right. It feels like something special is about to happen. And the people around you seem to support you and love what you're doing. It gives you wings when you feel you're creating something special. And, of course, when you are with your team and you're in this together, it makes it worth it. It creates something deeper.

When you are willing to make the sacrifices, and to do everything they ask of you—eat healthy, don't smoke, don't drink, have self-discipline, learn, participate, be hungry, train hard and smart, make the leap, have faith, go through pain and through failure, don't give in, don't give up, puke after training and then go for it again, do extra work, suffer, lead, motivate your teammates, be open, be honest, and start over from scratch—it will be worth it. Trust me.

Commitment

A pig and a chicken are walking down the road.

The chicken says: "Hey, pig, I was thinking we should open a restaurant!"

The pig replies: "Hmm, maybe, but what would we call it?"

The chicken responds: "How about *Ham-n-Eggs*?"

The pig thinks for a moment, and says: "No, thanks. I'd be committed, but you'd only be involved."

How involved are you? How committed are you to achieving your goal or your dream? Is it one moment in the day, or every minute, or every hour of the day?

Are you involved like the chicken, or committed like the pig? Do you want to be in the driver's seat, or in the back, enjoying the view? These questions are all coming at you. I decided, when I was gone from school, I would go all in for this project. I didn't have the best knowledge on how to do it, but I would listen and do anything they asked of me, and then 10% extra. I would write everything down, listen really carefully, and work on myself. I knew that if I wanted it, I could do it. I made a clear choice that this was the one thing: I would play on the best team in Belgium!! And I would make that happen! This was my mindset. It doesn't mean that I am the only one who made this team a successful team; I could feel that all the other players were like this. They were all thinking like this. I loved it. Every player believed that they were important to the team, in order that the team would be successful. They would be successful.

Doubt

Why is it that we doubt ourselves? It really is funny. As much as I was confident, I didn't have the slightest clue about how or what. But that was always the case; I have a strong self-belief. My father always said: "Strong in the head, my son. Strong in the head." And then he would grab my hair and shake it. I loved it when he did that. Also, because I had so much energy and had difficulty falling asleep when I was young, we developed a prayer, which I still use to this day. My father always asks: "Are you still doing your prayer, my son?" He taught it to me when I was young. My father would come lie next to me and say the prayer so I could learn it. I actually looked forward to that prayer; it gave space and rest in my head. After a busy day in the life of my younger self, after going to school, playing with my school friends, playing hockey...it was calming and soothing. One day, years later, I asked my dad, "Why did you teach me that prayer?" He said, "Because it was the only thing that made you calm." I suddenly realised that it was true. It made me calm. Here is the prayer:

In the name of the Father, the Son, and the Holy Spirit,
Jesus save me
Jesus protect me
Jesus help me
Bless us
Watch over us
Lead us
Feed us
Stay with us
Come into our heart
Enlighten our spirit
And let us never fight again
Teach me to love like you loved us
Teach me to have more patience
Teach me to be strong against evil
And open for good
Anything is possible with the help of Jesus Christ
Amen.

Whenever I would doubt, I would say this prayer. Before games, I say this prayer quickly in my mind, just before the whistle.

Sometimes you will have a dream that is just too big. It's a dream you get or a goal you want that is just too big to comprehend. People won't understand why you dream it, or why you want it. I remember I was in my room, and I felt so sad. I said, "Why me? Why do I feel these feelings? Why am I struggling? Why is it?" But I realised that it is normal. You can't comprehend everything. Sometimes life gives you challenges and dreams that are just too big, so that you can grow through it.

POSTULATE!

I wrote down on my wall, a year before I became a world champion, that I would be a world champion. I wrote down: "I am a world champion." And a year later, I was one.

Write down what you want to be. Close your eyes. Visualize yourself being it. Feel the feelings you would have.

I am……..

And see what happens.

**Don't just CONSUME,
CREATE!!
The world doesn't owe you
ANYTHING. You are here to create an
impact. You already have a voice.
TRAIN IT! You already have a body…
USE IT!!
You have GOD-GIVEN gifts, talents,
and abilities. Work at them every day.
Work on yourself. Focus on yourself.**

**I would LOVE to change THE
WORLD.
But, okay… I will change myself first.
Much harder!**

Chapter 3

My First Big Wakeup Call

Didn't Do My Best

When I was young, I often didn't do my best. I teased the teacher, and I made jokes with my classmates. Usually, when I felt I was under pressure, I started being distracted from the thing I was supposed to do. Even now, in high pressure moments, during a game or tournament, the hardest part in life or a game is to stay focused—on your growth, on your role or task—even when everything around you is hell. What are you going to do? Fall into the traps of distraction? Go off and lose focus on your goal and what you want to achieve? Because it seems too hard, or you're too tired? Listen to that voice in your head that says you can't do it? That blames the teacher for being bad? That blames the subject for being boring? Think of every reason for you not to work hard and go deeper? These things would happen to me. When you want to go to the highest level, in whatever you do, you'll end up with more and more moments like this. You learn it the hard way. In sports, at the highest level, it's very easy. When you're not fit, they'll replace you. There were times I would puke after a physical test because I ate a bit too late, and then would go back on the pitch to train again. It was mind over matter.

I grew up with a lot of opportunities: I went to the best school, had nice clothes, went on holidays, did several sports, and had lots of friends. Then came a point when I had to choose hockey or school. The options ran out. I had to choose, and it was very difficult. In either way, I had a feeling that I had big potential. I was labelled as a smart kid but not easy to handle. I was talented in several areas and was social. But it didn't seem that I was going places with my talents. People around me weren't satisfied with what I was doing, and that was very annoying. I knew I couldn't make everybody happy all the time, so I chose hockey. Why? Because something about that team pulled me. Also, the idea of going for the national team, and to be able to play at the Olympics, was a dream for me, and I knew somehow that I could do it.

I left school and went all in for hockey. It was also triggered by the fact that my school didn't take hockey seriously. In a fight, we separated. I never went back to that school. The big wakeup call came when I wasn't selected anymore for the national team. I had nothing going anymore—no friends, no hockey, no school. I got my school diploma by studying individually, and finished it. But my dream of being an Olympian was very far. Still, I had this belief somehow. I don't really know where it came from, but other people would call me crazy. I kept working hard on myself, and I kept controlling the things I could control. The only thing I focused on was myself and my game.

Criticize

"He has a right to criticize, who has a heart to help." – Abraham Lincoln

"Every time I go on the field, I give it my all, and if I'm not giving my 100%, I criticize myself." – Lebron James

It's very easy to be critical. But you would probably do the same if you were in his shoes. It's just a matter of changing perspective; and that is very hard, especially when you've never done it.

When you're on a team, it's very hard not to criticize. You are constantly together. On the field, you watch every move of your teammates. You wonder if they are eating well, living a healthy life, having enough sleep, focussing on becoming better, striving for excellence, and doing their best. You depend a lot on your teammates. You cannot afford someone having a bad day at the office. It could mean the difference between winning and losing, being world champion or Olympic champion, having a successful business or not, losing clients or winning clients, making or breaking a deal, or having a great idea or a shitty one—it's a very thin line, especially when you're under pressure.

When I go into criticizing mode, I tend to lose pleasure in my work. I lose my joy, but it makes me better. The biggest breakthroughs I have had as a player was when I acknowledged that I was not in my best form, and I went to players and staff members from my team and directly asked them what I could do better, to help not only myself but also others. It gave me a great sense of liberation in the way that it was okay to say I wasn't going great and needed help. Also, to ask not how they could help me but to ask how I could help them. It made me satisfied and gave me a great sense of purpose and energy. You notice that you are needed in this world, and that people actually see greatness in you, and that they often have great tips.

Happy Thoughts

"Change your thoughts and you change your world." – Norman Vincent Peale

I was playing a game in the Dutch championship. We had just lost the playoff semi-final, and we had to win in order to secure the third spot, to qualify for the European Hockey League. We drew in the last minute (1–1) and, therefore, had to play shootouts. Shootouts is much like in ice hockey, where you play a 1v1 against the keeper, starting from 25 metres.

I was reading the book on positive thinking, by Norman Peale. It said that whenever you doubt yourself, or you are going to do something you are unsure about, you say, "Everything is possible, with the help of Jesus Christ." As I also was reading a book about Jesus Christ, I kind of understand what Jesus is about. But don't get me wrong; I'm not an expert.

The other thing was that I missed a shootout against India in the quarter final of the World League final, a year from the World Cup, which will take place at the exact same venue. I was totally devastated after that tournament. I felt that I wasn't good enough, and that I didn't believe enough in myself; and that shootout was the drop. I did everything. I was the hardest worker but couldn't seem to let my team win at important moments.

Back to the shootout with my club, we lost the semi-final during playoffs of the Dutch League. We were devastated because we didn't achieve our goal. We lost confidence, and the team felt very heavy. We were a shadow of what we could be. It came to a shootout, and everybody on our team missed. You could tell that my teammates would miss in the way they were taking the shootouts. Sometimes you just see it. I had the same doubts and insecurities. There was a lot at stake here. This was the shootout series to win the game and play a sequel. And it was my first shootout after my missed one, a couple of months ago.

I did as it was written in the book by Norman Vincent Peale, and said several times to myself: "Everything is possible with the help of Jesus Christ. Everything is possible; everything is possible." I envisioned my shootout and what I was going to do. I practiced it several times, and in my movement, I had, again, three options, so I could anticipate what the keeper was doing. As I did my movement, I didn't have any stress, anxiety, or doubt, considering what was at stake: the rest of the team was missing their shootouts, and the guy who was normally taking my shootout didn't want to take it because he didn't have the self-confidence. I made my move and scored the goal! It was such an incredible feeling. I conquered my mind, and I scored. Happy thoughts are gold.

Self-discipline

I always felt that there was something there when I was young. I would have days when I would come home from school and immediately do my homework, and then relax. First, the effort, and then the relaxation. But I also remember that feeling and that voice: *Do it later; watch this movie and you'll feel good; go play ping pong; go look at your phone; watch videos all day; play games.* There were times when I was really into the flow of focus, and felt the pressure of studying but used the energy in a good way. Then I would become proud of myself that I was using all my intelligence and my God-given talents. And there were times when I would lose focus, and play videogames and watch television or social media all day. And you know this isn't the right thing to do; you just feel it! But you keep doing it. And I would feel myself slipping away in those bad habits again. Teachers would warn me, but I was ignorant.

Gratitude; forgiveness; meditation; active goal setting; healthy eating; sleep; exercise; organization; time management; persistence—Theodore Roosevelt once said that with self-discipline, most anything is possible. And Aristotle said, *"Good habits formed at youth make all the difference."*

You can achieve anything you want through self-discipline. But it's hard, and sometimes you don't achieve what you want. To let it go is maybe the best thing to do, but when you want to give up, you are often closer than you think. Most of the time, it's just a feeling. The most successful people had big failures but just didn't give up. It's important to learn from your mistakes. Either you win or you learn. There is no *lose*. I see people making the same mistakes over and over again. They just go on and cruise along, sleepwalking to the next crash, drinking the pain away, and not learning, or learning it the hard way. I've been like this, not wanting to see my shortcomings, criticizing others and not myself, not being disciplined, and letting myself go. But then I think about why I do it. I can create happiness through what I'm doing. I can make a difference in the world. And maybe, when I start making a small difference, others will follow.

But first, I need to grow. I need to have self-discipline to be of the biggest value to my team, my family, and everybody, and to learn continuously and to grow intentionally. And I need mentors, people who help me. I can't do it alone. That's why you need a team around you. Approach them, ask for help, and talk about your fears. Don't talk about your problems every day, because 90% don't care, and 10% are glad you have them. Tell people you want to learn and grow, and be disciplined about it. Share your goals and dreams. Ask what they see in you, and what you can improve. Ask them what your shortcomings are. Talk about it because, before you know it, life hits you from the blind side, with stuff you can't anticipate, and stuff you can't imagine. And then, when you're unprepared, life can be hard! It can break you, get you on your knees, and keep you there permanently.

Suffering

"Human progress is neither automatic nor inevitable... Every step toward the goal of justice requires sacrifice, suffering, and struggle; the tireless exertions and passionate concern of dedicated individuals."
– Martin Luther King

You'll suffer. Every great thing wasn't built by people doing nothing. The brothers Wright: Do you know that they weren't the only ones trying to invent a way to fly in the air? There were teams with a lot of money, who had a lot more resources. The brothers Wright just had a bicycle shop, but they had discipline and energy, and they formed a great team. They failed every day with their experiments, but they believed so strongly that it was possible to get back up after every setback. Until they succeeded, they kept going.

Anyhow… Buildings, economy, peace, love: When you look at some of the stories of people who had great success, or who achieved something in their time, where no one was doing what they were doing, they had grit and discipline. They suffered, but they continued when they were tired. They started where they were. When they wanted to give up, they didn't, because they knew there was something—something bigger than themselves. Every time you go out of your comfort zone, feeling awkward and afraid of the unknown, tap into your greatness. It requires suffering, but you are able to push through. Feel the pain and suffer, but do it anyhow. That's when you grow. When you feel unstoppable and limitless, life then can become an adventure. There is also a difference between mental and physical suffering. You'll be hurt by everyone, even people you love. That may be what hurts the most. But that's just part of life. Deal with it. Push through. Or get some help. When I first started going to the gym, I couldn't even do 50 pushups. Now I can do thirty bench presses, with 85 kg. Still, it was nothing much compared to professional weightlifters. But I had to start small. I had to start where I was. Doing ten pushups, 3 times, was already hard in the beginning. But I believed, through hard work, dedication, and consistency, I would get there, because others have done it before me. That leads me to say that leaders are so important. In order to do something, some people need to see somebody else doing it. But what if only one person sees it, and the rest don't. What if only one guy on the team knows what to do and believes in it so hard, but the rest just don't do it because they haven't seen it. As Eleanor Roosevelt said, *"The future belongs to those who believe in the beauty of their dreams."*

Saw All My Failures

There was a point in my life where I had big time troubles. I was in my room and was lying on my bed. I had just left school and had started individual learning, and my mind was all on hockey, but I wasn't selected for the national team. I felt I was really tested because, for the first time in my life, it only came down to me—no more teachers and classmates. If I didn't do anything, nothing would happen. I regretted that I wasted some of my opportunities. But there was also a voice in me that said, "Go for your dream. Come on, start. Show everyone what you have."

I got a personal trainer, Majid, and asked for help to make me an athlete. And then I just started doing everything in my power with what I had, to be the best player I could be, with the knowledge I had at that time on how to do it. In my eyes, it was just working and running as hard as I could, and attacking! Approach the play. Go for it. Take risks. I've got nothing to lose. And so I went, and I ended up on the national team before I knew it. Coaches started believing in me. Players around me started getting energy from me. I was becoming a player on that field, who could have an impact on winning the game. From then on, it clicked that I was accountable for how my team functioned.

When you hold yourself accountable, everything changes. It will become clear that your failures were designed by your hand. No one else was accountable for your failures. Putting that mirror in front of you is hard, but when you start working on yourself—learning from your failures, writing your goals down, and having faith that you can change your failures into opportunities—your disasters turn into miracles. Buddhism says that with the end of one universe, another one begins. Western people have a tendency to believe more in an apocalyptic end. Or that the apocalypse already arrived. I believe that every end is the beginning of something new, and that failure is inevitable on your way to your goal or dream. You will have to forgive yourself from time to time. Be gentle with yourself. As Gandhi said, *"In the end, everything will be okay; if it's not okay, it's not the end."*

As in a hockey game, you can make mistake after mistake. You can have a missed pass or a missed occasion. You have small failures, in your eyes. But rebooting your mind and thinking about the next action, and going back to your true self, will make you prepare for future plays and opportunities during the game. As it is in life, too many of us quit when they meet failure. They think they haven't found something they like. I can tell you that I liked playing hockey. But at some point, you will have to grow, even in the areas in which you once thought you were talented and you were the best.

Of course, we tend to get comfortable. We tend to settle and stop stretching. We stop growing, and we stop learning, or we have a win and we think that we're there, and that now the world and the universe owes us something. Nobody, and nothing, owes you anything. I had moments, during a game, when I was frustrated about my level, and then I would force play or complain against my teammates and referees. My focus went from internal to external. I was more concerned about what other people around me were doing, rather than focusing on myself, my feelings, my thoughts, my emotions, my progress, and my play.

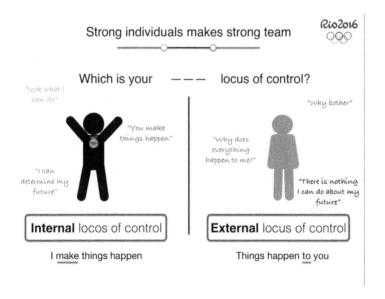

Strong individuals makes strong team   Rio 2016

Which is your — — — locus of control?

"Look what I can do"

"You make things happen"

"Why bother"

"Why does everything happen to me?"

"I can determine my future"

"There is nothing I can do about my future"

Internal locos of control | **External** locus of control

I make things happen | Things happen to you

This is something that really helps me, on and off the pitch. It puts the focus on yourself, and makes it clear and simple in complex situations where you should focus and go for it.

Get a PERSONAL TRAINER. Or a MENTOR. Or anyone who is a master in their field. Majid helped me become a BEAST. You need someone to look at you from a different perspective. Listen to his advice. He is an expert. Don't just go to the gym and think there will be a magical spray which will make you unstoppable. It takes blood, sweat, tears, and... DATA! @Polar.

Eat natural food while you are at it. J And lots of porridge and proteins. Vegetables are also very tasty. I like broccoli. And water. Drink water!! But not too much coffee. It makes you go bonkers. Let's go!!

Chapter 4

Good Mistakes

A good mistake is a mistake on which you can build. A mistake can be your greatest teacher.

Judging

It's in my nature to judge. We see it all around us. People make a program on judging sports, politics, or other subjects. It's easy to judge, and to have an opinion. The hardest part is to create something, to manifest your greatness or to bring solutions to the table. I've had people judge me that I wasn't good enough, several times. Or I judged my teammates that they were lazy or not focused. In fact, they were doing their very best, but only in the way in which they thought was the best way. A lot of times, we judge from our world: how we grew up and how we were raised, with our beliefs and values engrained in our brains and hearts. We project them onto others, but maybe, in their little world, they are doing exactly the things they ought to be doing. Therefore, judging other people, and in my case, teammates, can be a very tricky thing.

I've noticed that when I judge, I'm the biggest fool. Because, in that way, I create a big distance between me and my teammates, friends, or family… especially in sports, where the minute the whistle blows, you should be free of judging, because you can't lose energy. I feel then that I play with a heavy backpack, and it weighs on me. See every

49

human being or player as a whole human. Don't judge him. I've noticed, when I consciously believe more in myself and in others, the world changes: Creativity grows, and fun grows. I feel, when I judge after a bad play, it then influences my future plays. Maybe I have a great goal waiting, or a great action, or a nice give and go. But when I hold onto that judging—and most of the time, it's negative—and maybe, even if sometimes I'm right—it holds me back! When I judge, I think then that that person did something wrong, and in order for me to function properly, that person must change or go.

I noticed that when I change myself, the world changes, and my relation to the other person changes. And my life is better; I enjoy it more. I'm not holding a grudge, and I'm open for new and different experiences, which doesn't mean that that voice of judging and giving opinions stays. I think sometimes there are people that do really bad things: people that hurt you, cheat on you, lie to you, and have different agendas. Finding a balance in knowing that's just how people are, and changing how you deal with it, changes everything.

Not Talking

Balance is needed between not talking and talking too much. I find it difficult to sometimes talk about the hard stuff, or to talk about small stuff. I like to go hard, working on something, all together, until the breaking point, and then growing and feeling I am part of something bigger than daily life, having a dream or a goal that I wouldn't think possible. I learned it the hard way that talking is sometimes very important. My first girlfriends were really tortured by me. I just didn't know what to say. Talking about how I felt, and what I was thinking, was difficult for me. Still, now, it's uncomfortable for me to talk about what I'm thinking or feeling. I get a weird feeling when I think about saying what I am thinking or feeling during a meeting. It's very strange. But then, when I do talk, and it comes out, I feel much lighter and have much more energy. It's also the fact that you overcome the fear of saying what's on your mind. When I was young, I was with a girl. One of her friends asked me if I would like to be with her. Of course, I said yes. And so, the girlfriend went to the girl and said that I said, "Yes." The funny thing was that I just didn't know what to say, and she broke up with me. I was afraid of talking, and just had no clue about what she wanted or how to approach her. I think I was like 12 years old. But I had the confidence and self-belief that it would come. I just had to have some patience. I couldn't expect myself to go all in from the first day.

So we drove back on our bicycles from school, and came to a point where we had to go different ways. Then I would just drive off and yell, "See you tomorrow!" In my head, there were a million options: *What should I do? Should I stop and kiss her? How would that go? Just kiss her at once, or wait and talk? What should I talk about then?* And before I knew it, I yelled from a distance, driving away, "See you tomorrow!" And I would think, "You stupid! You just go away without talking or saying anything?!" Now that I think about it, it's pretty funny, because if you saw me now, you would think that I'm an extroverted person. But when it comes to girls, I can be very shy and insecure. There's something about women that I admire and respect in a very big way.

No Confidence

To have success, you need confidence. But how do you get confidence? I've had points where I didn't believe in myself. People around me got me back up. When you look at your life and look at where you are now—when you look at all the horrors you've faced, the challenges you've overcome, the fears you've looked in the eye, the mountains you've climbed, the bridges you've built, the people you've met, the lives you've helped to get better, the people you've inspired, the energy that was needed to achieve what you've achieved—and you're still here—you survived. You can take confidence out of that.

As an athlete, you train yourself every day. You stretch your muscles. You experiment on trainings. You push yourself. You're in pain. You grow where it hurts. Improve yourself daily. Develop skills that you expand on the training field. You run for yourself and your teammates, and for your family and the name on your back; you want to give pride. Only when you do it consciously, in this way, you create confidence. You know what you can do because you did it before.

Once I had to give a presentation about our Olympic journey, on how we were such a great team. Two companies were in the midst of a joint venture, so they wanted to know how we, as a team with two cultures, French and Dutch, came together, and how we did it. They wanted to hear our story on how to bring people closer together so you can have that extra 10%, where individuals grow bigger then themselves through teamwork. It doesn't happen with every team, but when it happens, it's magic! I had never done a presentation about this subject that was close to my heart. But I accepted it. I would figure out the "how," later. I knew the "why." It was for my family and my teammates, and what they meant to me; it was why I would run harder with them on the pitch. It was how my team gives me wings and lifts me up when I'm down, and lifts me higher when I'm up.

I went to someone professional who could help me learn how to give a presentation, and when I go for something, I go all the way. I practiced it; I did my presentation over and over again. I implemented every tip people gave me on how to become better at it. I looked for inspiration everywhere, and I listened carefully. It was awkward and uncomfortable, but I set a goal and went for it. Then, when I was going to the event, I wasn't really informed on how many people would be there. I had only heard about giving presentations to small groups of people. So I expected a bit of the same. I was on my way with my dad to the event. He didn't know how well prepared I was for this presentation, so he was giving me tips, up until I looked him in the eyes and said: "Dad, I've got this. Stop giving me stress."

As we went through the door, we came into a cinema complex. Little did I know that the companies I was presenting to had 400 employees, and they were all sitting there. The screen was as big as any screen in a cinema. So my presentation was huge. I saw people at the top in the complex, like ten of them, on panels, with computers and headsets for the lights and sound, because someone was busy giving a big presentation. It was Jef Staes, a big name in the industry. There was someone who pointed out that we had to go all the way down to the first row, to sit there and wait until it was my turn. There I sat with my dad and my Olympic silver medal, and my mind map, which I learned to do whilst reading a book about it, by Tony Buzan. And my dad was giving his tips. It was a funny situation when I think about it. I could have blacked out, giving in to my fear. I could have run out, and said, "This is too big for me." But wait a minute; I prepared for it. I went to a professional. I had myself prepared. And if I failed, just as in sports, I would go back and work on myself and learn and improve. That's how winning is done. But I nailed it. I focused on what I wanted to say. It was not just me. It was the story of the team, and how we came together and achieved a dream.

Not Learning

It's hard to learn *when* to learn. You sometimes don't know it, but the biggest lessons are right in front of your nose. You just can't see it. You're cruising through life, making the same mistakes, again and again. What I had to change, when something or someone hurt me in a way, was to see that it often was a present. For example, when my girlfriend says that I'm not communicating well, I say, "Well, yeah, that's because I'm tired. I don't feel like communicating. The deeper reason is that I don't want to change, because I know, in order to change or grow, I need to invest in myself, and that is sometimes really painful because you'll see your flaws again, and you'll go into some areas of your life where you don't want to go.

Teams, when they fail, or athletes, often have these habits. You have guys on the team that shut down, and go to their beds and say nothing anymore about the game or the failure. You have guys going out in the city to the bar, hoping to forget the pain and failure, which will come back in the end. Talking about it, reliving the moment, and going through it step-by-step is when you learn. For me, that's when I look at my images, or when I look back at the game and watch with an open mind, seeing opportunities and possibilities that I didn't see or know during the game: how I could optimize my positioning; how I could talk to my player in front of me, and have better, sharper positioning.

During a pool game in a tournament where we had to qualify for the Olympics, one of my teammates shouted at me in an aggressive way, as though he was really angry that I would intentionally not pass him the ball. I just didn't see him; I was focused on getting the ball to another area of the field. I felt that it was still in the air after the game. We are together for a long time; we are in the hotel for a couple of weeks, and we have a lot of meetings, so you can have a lot of interactions. So, you can notice pretty quickly when you feel a distance between you and a team member. Even just talking to him becomes a challenge, and uncomfortable. But, as Susan Jeffers' book says, *"Feel the fear and do it anyhow."* I went to him with the team computer. We have a couple of computers with a database of every game of the opposition, and our games as well. In this way, you can watch your own games and really improve your play. When you watch every game, you can almost predict everything that is going to happen when you play that team.

Anyway, I went to him and showed him the clip. The adrenaline was going through my veins because I did know what to expect. The last time we had contact was when he shouting at me. It couldn't get any worse... But he started explaining what he had in his head and what he wanted to do once he got the ball, and he explained that he was struggling because he didn't get many balls during the game. So we had a constructive talk, and I felt great. I understood where he was coming from and could frame his outburst. So this was a big learning experience. I never had this before with a player. Still, we have our little moments. But at least we know how to solve them.

Procrastinating

So, I left school on Fridays with a bunch of homework. The teacher just finished with saying not to forget to start my homework on time. A voice inside me said, "Wow, what if I finished my homework now so I could watch movies tonight, go to the hockey game on Saturday, sleep over with one of my friends, play on Sunday, and return home, knowing that I can sleep comfortably on time, and maybe sit in the living room for some time, because I know I'm prepared for Monday." Everything would be done. But then, three days later, I would find myself with nothing done, and stressing out because, along the way, during the week, I had had that same voice with preparing everything on time, but it seemed I didn't fill in my *task section* in my agenda, where you could see every task you would have to complete, or any upcoming tests. What happened with those great ideas of doing the productive stuff first, and having everything in order?

This did not happen once, but it happened every time. It would be a big time mess because I had to do everything last minute. I had to call classmates to complete my paperwork and send me through notes during playtime, learning my Latin words just before going into class. It would work out, but I would feel guilty and bad because I didn't really get the most out of it. Procrastinating is a very bad habit for achieving what you want. Don't start now, or today. You'll have time, somewhere tomorrow, or somewhere next week.

Apparently, after hearing a TED talk by Tim Urban, it's the monkey-mind taking over. It's when you are working on some deadline or project, and suddenly, you find yourself scrolling your Instagram page and asking yourself why you end up with your phone in your hand. Or when you end up in front of the refrigerator just after you said you were going to answer all of your emails. Or when you end up all sweaty and exhausted from a three-hour ping pong marathon with your brother, and feeling guilty when you go back behind your books or whatever thing you need to get done. The guilty feeling would get in, and you feel like a fool because that energy you lost could have been easy. Or when you just had a team meeting, and you find yourself playing fifa again for three hours, forgetting about the content of what was said.

Monkey-mind; beware of the monkey. Kill it if you have to. Listen to that voice that all of us have, which tells you the right direction. Focus and work on your ideas, dreams, or goals.

Vulnerability

It's not easy to form trust. You need vulnerability for that; not that you have to cry every time you speak, or share your problems every time: 90% don't care, and 10 % are glad you have them. But on a team, it's different. You are all together. You're going to the battlefield together. You'll have to give your life for the other. But when something is holding you back, you'll feel frustration, lack of energy, lack of passion, lack of focus, and lack of sharing the same values and goals in the functioning of the team. And you end up frustrated. You don't get the results you want. The team is not going your way. You can see the problem, but you can't see the solution.

Only when you give it your 100%, you may be able to help others or criticize others. Confronting difficult issues takes courage. It's like fish under the table... You can't see them, but you can smell them. And they stink big time!! Nasty! And you feel a nagging feeling, something that just isn't right. And to go deep in, it takes energy and time— making time, or having time, and then channelling your energy on the right things—something that is rare these days. It's hard when you're in a team where there is no vulnerability.

Al gore says, *"As human beings, we are vulnerable to confusing the unprecedented with the improbable. In our everyday experience, if something has never happened before, we are generally safe in assuming it is not going to happen in the future, but the exceptions can kill you."* Brené Brown says that *"vulnerability is the birthplace of connection, and the path to the feeling of worthiness. If it doesn't feel vulnerable, the sharing is probably not constructive."*

We have all had dads who look very firm and steady, and who are the role models we want them to be, or who we think they ought to be—working hard, earning tough money. But the truth is that I want my father as he is, with all the shortcomings and failures he had in his life. I'm not saying that he didn't have successes, but he probably had some things that didn't turn out as he would like. When you show that vulnerability, you'll actually notice that quite a lot of people care about you and support you.

I had one moment where I cried in front of the team when I talked about my red card. I put away the emotions for a long time, but we lost the tournament before the Olympics because of that. It came to me that I had a big part in it. When we had a team workshop for media training, after the *red card tournament*, every player could pick two nasty questions for the player sitting next to him. The man leading the workshop would ask these questions and would go deep on you. You, as a player, would have to give a clear and sound answer. But when he started over the red card, which happened a few weeks earlier, I started crying. And then Felix came to me and the coach, and they said they actually appreciated that moment. I felt very embarrassed and very vulnerable. It was special because Felix said that he thought I didn't really care… but I really did. This team was my life; I would do anything.

GO for GOLD!!!!

The rest is boring as hell.

Chapter 5

My Family

Support

I feel that my family is my biggest support in achieving my dreams and goals. They are the ones who believe the most in my capabilities. You don't get to choose your family, and that is, in my eyes, very special. You know each other from day one, and have the possibility to know each other till the end of life. Of course, you see families where challenges, situations, or problems break family bonds. Families get in the grip of negative situations and are likely to separate or get into fights.

It can also be that family members start to have different beliefs and values than others. It is important then to remember the things that bring families together, rather than to look for the things that separate us. That made me think about the role of the family in our society, and if it should be something to strive for. A lot of people give up. In a divorce, the children may blame one of the parents for it, which has the consequence that they don't talk for years, or even have to go to court to get things sorted. It is a terrible experience for both children and parents because, in the end, they all love each other. There could be a family dispute, where one lends money to the other, and the other can't pay it back. Or a moment where a family member gets a higher position in the family business or does a better job.

There are so many challenges and circumstances you can't anticipate, which makes it important to know the core of a family. What is your family about? What do you want to get out of it? Where can you have added value, and what are you doing to help others achieve their dreams and goals? The love my parents gave me has had a great impact on what I am now, and on the challenges I keep overcoming for who I want to be. Now I can tell the difference between me and others. Where others give up and stop learning, I feel I have an extra edge or an extra mile in me.

But there are also examples of people ending up in a bad family situation, and they still turn out great because they learned to overcome big challenges at a very young age. They were tested and came out stronger, maybe with a lot more struggle or emotional pain. There are also kids too spoiled by their families, who don't succeed. It is a very complex thing. It's like in anything: What makes a singer great? What makes Messi great? What makes Oprah great? Or Nelson Mandela? What makes Jay Z great? What made Jesus great? What does it take to have that special thing? To nail it? It also depends on what works for you.

My parents had big fights. I remember seeing my mother cry once. It was the worst thing ever. But love always prevails. That is the goal. I also remember my mother stands for talking to the bone, and leaving no stone unturned. She would talk about everything. Well, there are some areas you don't really need to talk about, if you know what I mean. They teach us to be, and to give love. After my love bucket is full again, I can go back into the jungle, where I can get hurt, wrestle with jaguars, fight with snakes, tangle with crocodiles, kill bricks, dance with orangutans, fight off diseases, and become king of the jungle. Or at least die trying.

I believe in quality over quantity. You could have five hours of the worst Christmas party, with all kinds of taboos, weird looks, and frustration, while at the same time, you could have one hour of the best Christmas party you've ever had, where you talk about your adventures, dreams and goals, and heartbreaks and new loves. Or you can tell each other the truth, without ego stepping in the way and jinxing the party. It can be a wonderful place, full of wonder and miracles. That's what my family means to me.

Safe Harbour

When I was young, we would go on family trips to Greece, on a sail boat. We would go from island to island, from crystal blue waters to white sandy beaches. Those were the days. Heaven does exist. You just have to open your eyes! Like Samos or Skorpios, the island Onassis bought but is now owned by a Russian billionaire, oligarch Dmitry Rybolovlev, who is also the current owner of the football club, AS Monaco. Manolis, a dear friend of my father, who lived in Greece, rented his sail boat to us. And now, he actually works with my father in his business, Diplomatic Card Company. It is a business that invented the tax- free fuel card and the VAT card for diplomats. Diplomats can buy tax-free goods. Since the Vienna Convention on diplomatic relations in 1964, my father digitalized the market for the diplomats. It has been a very hard and long run, as the digitalizing momentum in Belgium isn't quite there. We are rather conservative. We like to stay in our little comfort zones, rather than to shake it all up into a new, bright, digitalized future, where people will no longer have to do silly paperwork but can live!!

But back to the family trip, sailing in Greece. On one day, I remember, it was stormy, with big waves and strong winds. It was the type of weather at sea where you feel the power of nature. It is so majestic and big that it makes you feel small, but on the other hand gives you a feeling of, "Is this all you've got? Give me more!" You can picture yourself, together with Columbus, exploring the ocean, standing all the way at the tip where the waves crash against the boat, and the water splashes against your body, driven by the heavy wind. There are some who are scared, and others who become fearless and take it on like their part of the storm.

Sorry, but I keep losing my focus of the story. So, there was a storm coming, and my family had to find a safe harbour to avoid the storm. We found one on a little island. And in that little harbour, there were no waves or wind whatsoever. You were at peace. A family is like this. My family is wonderful. Every time I go back to my family, my self-esteem rises, and my batteries recharge. It's a bit like Wall-E, when he hits the sun with his rechargeable solar panels and recharges his batteries in an instant.

Believe!

We are at an interesting point now with our family. My brother went to London and followed his heart. He then did his thesis about the diplomatic market being the biggest in Europe, with an estimation of 22,000 diplomats, the unsung peacemakers of our world. He believed deep down that he would be able to make it, and now he is making it happen. He launched a tax-free fuel card for diplomats, the first digital tax-free fuel card for diplomats in history, revolutionizing the diplomat market.

The same goes for when I went for this hockey dream: in the history of Belgium, it had never happened that a team was able to win a medal (except for the water polo team, in 1920, in Stockholm). Believing in something that has never happened before is also the same for entrepreneurs. In some way, it's for everyone. You are born, and then you grow up to be someone you were never before. You don't know who you are going to be in a few decades.

Will you be successful, or end up broke and unhappy, believing in no other option? Or will you be someone who achieved every goal and dream you ever wanted? Or will you have to settle at one point? You don't know. Still, what I believe defines my behaviour. Do I listen to my feelings, telling me I'm tired and I don't feel like getting up? Or that I don't feel like moving forward or putting in the work needed to move forward? Or that I don't feel like learning from my past mistakes? Even just thinking about them makes me sick, especially the feeling that maybe I was thinking wrongly and I had to have a different attitude; and especially when you think about the fact that you are the creator of your own destiny.

Is it then not horrific to think that the circumstances I'm in at this very moment of my life, the things I feel and think, the time I have and the things I do, are all on me? Not the teacher I thought treated me wrongly; not the trainer who was shitty; not the friends who talked behind my back? Not the bad weather? Not the horrific boss? Not the sickness I have? Not the bad performances I keep having again and again and again? Not the fights I have? Is it all on me? Well, you better believe that you are the creator of your own destiny, and that you can have at least a big impact on how your life will unfold. What unspoken dreams are you holding for yourself? What people did you wrong and are still in your system as clutter or mud, and are slowing down your growth? What beliefs are holding you down? They could be beliefs like, "It's too hard;" "I can't do it;" "I'm too tired;" "It's not worth it;" "The world doesn't need me."

Writing this first book is exciting because most of the stuff I'm writing flows right out of me, without any hesitation. Most of the stuff is already inside me; I'm just writing it down and, therefore, I'm deliberately showing myself on paper what is going on inside my head. It's pretty scary sometimes, but when you write it down, it's real. And you can consciously reshape things, or become aware of what you think and feel, which implacably influences how you view the world and universe, and how far you can influence the world in a positive way by becoming free, from the inside. When you're stressed, you project stress. When you're excited, you will project excitement onto others. When you believe so hard in what needs to happen, you will form a behaviour that meets that belief, and you will inflict belief onto others. You will have powers. You will be able to give confidence to others. It's easy to believe when others believe. What do you do when you have to walk the lonely road, where your belief is tested, and where you meet resistance and pain? What do you do then? Do you continue, or throw in the towel? Do you use the pain to push you to greatness?

Faith

"Faith is taking the first step, even when you don't see the whole staircase." – Nelson Mandela

Sometimes, in life, you need to take the first step, but you don't really know where it's going, even though you can feel it in your bones that it is the right thing to do. But it scares you, because you're doing something others may not have the courage for. Or they're paralysed by fear of failure, or fear of success. What if it works out and you can't handle it? When I wasn't selected for the national team (and basically, what it means is that you are no longer on the team, and you don't have to come to training sessions, etc.), the Olympic dream and World Cup dream stopped, in an instant.

But I continued to train hard; I went on doing extra sessions. When I had to do 10 shuttles, I did 12. When we had to do the beep test, I went on until I puked. I stopped eating candy, and I only drank water. I took my shakes, went to a personal trainer, rested on time, and cancelled my social life. I went all in on hockey. Remember, this was at the point when I wasn't selected. There was something inside me that drove me and pushed me, and made me come back again and again and again, until I made it happen, and until every club team wanted me on their team. This was because of my perseverance, and not giving up on my dream. Don't let anyone tell you that you can't do it. It's not their dream; it's yours!

I also felt I was good at it, and that I could go further. I had big potential; I could see it and feel it. I know I wasn't where I should be, but I had the vision. I could see myself on the team. And it's easy. Sometimes people say to me it's so hard, but there are simple targets to attain. When you normally make 3 goals, 5 good passes, 3 tackles, and 5 ball losses in a game, try and double those numbers during training. Like the United States Marine Corps principle says, *"Train like you fight."* The same is for athletes; or even for salesmen, doctors, or performers at every other level. Some people don't see it, but they perform, most of the time, exactly the same way at training as in games.

That's why you train: to get all that stuff out, and so that it becomes second nature during games. When you fail to prepare, you prepare to fail. It's very simple. Take the best performer you know. Maybe Lukaku is a good example. He is currently one of the best, if not the best, strikers Belgium has ever had. He has a drive that comes from the inside, not from the outside. He has faith in his own abilities and in his own powers. He believed so strongly in himself that he came back, even when Mourinho benched him at Chelsea. He got knocked down, but he came back. And he's killing it.

Preachers

Rudi Mannaerts is someone I go and listen to very often. Even after a game, on Sunday, I go with my father to listen to his preaching. He cleans my soul when he talks. Whenever I lose faith—and that will happen, trust me—I go and look for inspiration. And he is one that speaks from the heart, to the heart. In every one of us, there is a preacher—a greater voice that resonates with everyone; a voice that unites, not divides; a voice that gives strength to those who truly listen.

When we were playing the EHL final Bloemendaal season, 2017-2018, it was half time, and we were 2–0 down against the national champions, Kampong. They were the current European champions. We were playing okay the first half, like we always did. A week earlier, we lost in three games against Amsterdam. We won the first one with shootouts, but we lost the second one when we were 2–0 up, with 20 minutes to go. Amsterdam came back and won on shootouts. The third game, they had a bigger momentum than us, and we couldn't get out of our negative spiral. We were devastated: best team in the league, with the biggest names, and we didn't even reach the final.

Kampong eventually won the playoffs and became Dutch national champions, winning against Amsterdam. So, back to the European Final. We were 2–0 down against the Dutch Champions, Kampong. But then we went into the dressing room. Michel takes his time before speaking to the team. Normally, he chooses his points, and then, at the end, when he gets into it, he starts projecting a lot of energy to the team. He was shouting out from the depth of his lungs: "I want you to be RUTHLESS!!" While repeating this 5 or more times, he was smashing with all his force onto the orange little stool where his tactic board was lying. He was smashing it so hard, and several times, while yelling, "Ruthless," that he put a dent in the stool.

We went out to the pitch and won the game 6–2. Xavi Lleonart roofed the first goal with a backhand so hard. I hadn't seen him hitting the backhand that hard the whole year. We truly transcended as a team. We had a fire burning inside that was just unstoppable, and we won at our own club Bloemendaal. We eventually made it after being in a low place, to transcend our own level. When you have the courage to say the right things, at the right moments, in front of the people you want to talk to, life can be a wonderful thing.

GOOD to GREAT to PHENOMENAL

Chapter 6

Sick and Tired of Myself

Who Do You Want To Be?

Not what, but who. While writing this chapter down, I didn't really know what to expect. It's not easy to answer this question. Now I am this hockey player, every day, getting up for that dream, working hard, and making our nation proud. The thing I like the most, when I walk onto a pitch or work floor, is when I start to feel that I am part of something bigger than just myself, and that I am willing to give it my all and to go all out for what it is I want. And what I want is to contribute to everyone—not only seek my own good but the good for everyone. As it says in Corinthians, Chapter 10, Verse 23, *"Everything is permissible, but not everything is beneficial. Everything is permissible, but not everything builds up."* This is something that someone said to me in the *Get Your Book Done* workshop, in London, after I asked Raymond about bad thoughts. As he explained that the postulates and intentions you have influence your physical world, and that things will come to you, and not the other way around, I asked him what to do with bad thoughts because, sometimes, I have some bad thoughts, and then I can feel it. And I feel bad that I have those thoughts.

I don't really remember what he answered, but during the break, a man came up to me and, apparently, he was curious to find an answer to my question. Because he suddenly came up to me, even though I had never met him, and then said that he might have a good answer to my question, joy and happiness suddenly filled my body. I threw a question out to the universe, and then there came a man I never met, solving my question. He said he looked some things up on the internet, and then came up with the part from the bible about Corinthians, Chapter 10, Verse 23. It opened my mind, and it was so wonderful.

All thoughts are permissible. Not all are beneficial. So, what is beneficial? Synonyms of beneficial are *advantageous, favourable, helpful, useful*… For example, in sports, defending really well is very beneficial for your team. Living a professional life outside the pitch is very beneficial for your team, and not only for your team but for everyone. Therefore, I ask myself, every day, if the actions I undertake are beneficial to me, my family, my team, my physical health, my mental health… Am I growing? Am I contributing to the bigger picture? Am I only doing what is good for me, or also what is good for others? Am I someone who dares to take risks, to accept failure and to learn from those failures? Someone who overcomes doubt and hardship, who is strong enough to pursue his dreams and goals, and who takes his people along the way? Someone who dares to take the first step, even when I can't see the whole staircase?

You buckle up and go, and take the leap, so when you're old, you'll have no regrets. Whether my goal is to create a family business, a digital platform, an app—or anything—just do it. Success isn't something that hits me in my sleep. It's possible to have a moment of enlightenment to make me start the journey, but the journey to success is long, and it's hard. It will beat me to my knees and keep me there permanently if I let it. I will have setbacks. But every setback is a setup for a comeback. And when I want to lead, I'll lead with all my struggles and scars. I won't make people think I'm some kind of special supernatural superhero. I'm a human being, just like anyone else. I have doubts, but I just know how to handle them and override them with huge positivity.

Self-reflection

Who do you want to be? Who do I want to be? What do I want to get out of this life? What goals and dreams do I want to achieve? What values and beliefs are important to me? Is it money that drives me? Or is it fame, or is it the opinions of others? Do I have the courage to listen to my inner voice? All these questions drive me crazy sometimes, and give me anxiety at night. Am I doing it right? What's my vision of myself in ten years? Right now I have a very clear vision of who I want to be in the national team and my hockey team Bloemendaal. I want to be of a world class level. I want to go from good to great, to unstoppable, being the best I can be. I know this will be hard, but I'm willing to take the steps needed. I'm willing to look in the mirror and change myself, or transform. I'm willing to be open to other visions or opinions. I'm willing to learn. I'm willing to give it my all and expect nothing in return. I'm willing to bring out my soul, my heart, and my body on that pitch. I'm willing to read the books and to act on my ideas. I'm willing to experiment.

I know I have a lot to learn; I know that I have ignorance—I can go on and on, but I think I made myself clear. While I'm writing this, I feel my focus becoming bigger, and my energy flowing more and more in the lines I write. I feel that this way of thinking gives me opportunity and makes me open. It opens my heart. It is truly incredible what it can bring you by having some self-reflection. Also, what I've learned is to ask someone what it is they see in me. It can be very enlightening. What are the strengths you show to other people, and how are they helping them?

Thoughts

Thoughts define what you are and what you do. They create the universe around you. Have you ever had it happen where you thought about something and it popped up in your life? Like you were thinking about someone, and then suddenly they call. So, what if I'm conscious about my thoughts? I can choose them, and by choosing them, my day will be a day full of miracles. This is only if you are open to how wonderful life is. Today, I went to Amsterdam after a day's work at DCC, my dad's company. I drove to Amsterdam to have a coffee with Pepijn, from the Bloemendaal board. It was a 1.5 hour drive, and I listened to Raymond's audio on the way there. His lesson was about the importance of cleaning up all the messes in your life—from the mess in your closets to the mess in some of your relationships. Every person who starts cleaning their messes starts with around 15–20 messes. I, on this day, have 15. When you start to be conscious about your messes, you start to see messes everywhere. So the journey will be long, but I'll get there.

So, back to Pepijn. We came together just to share our thoughts about the past season and the new season, and how things were changing, and what to focus on. It was a good talk at Anna Haen, a nice place in Abcoude. Actually, it is some kind of barn, transformed into an eat and drink place, where you can have company events and reserve meeting rooms. We communicated effectively. It's interesting what happens when you shut down ego and are open to new ideas, suggestions, and even negative feedback. You can learn so much from one talk. So, a very good feeling and excitement was created.

I was looking forward to a new season, with the new players coming and the old leaving. It was a very good mix of young and old, which can give a very exciting dynamic. Then I drove to Krammerstraat, to our apartment, where a lot of good memories were based, and a lot more were to come. I packed to go to David Lloyd, to have a small gym session to get the body back in top shape for the new season with Bloemendaal, and the kick off with Bloemendaal. So, I felt great! Everything was going awesome. It was a good day. Every project I was doing had my attention. Then I came home, and I opened a few letters… and boom, the good feeling was gone.

There were some bills I had to pay, which I didn't know about, such as bills for the water. There were also some other bills that were new to me because of the fact that this was the first time living on my own, with some other guys, and I had to take responsibility in areas that were new to me. The thoughts can then get negative, because it's a lot of money you have to pay, and you want to use that money for other stuff. But, oh well, this life can knock you down; and if you're not careful, it can knock you down on your knees and keep you there permanently.

Then I wanted to watch a good movie to relax, but I couldn't find the TV remotes. Then the Wi-Fi didn't work. These are very small problems, but still, after a hard day, you look forward to a little me-time. The point I'm trying to make is that when you lose the bigger perspective, and start seeing the small stupid things taking over your mood and mindset, that's where you start losing. When you know what you want, and you have that focus and are able to hold those positive thoughts, positive things can happen. And you'll start making plans to solve those problems, and you'll see that for every problem, there is a solution!

The BIGGEST freedom comes with DISCIPLINE

No Mistakes Possible

What if I told you that you only had one chance—only one moment where that person you want to impress comes into your life? What if you, in that moment, fail? What if you are not given a second chance, because there is someone else filling up your space? And it's all over, playing the Olympic final in Rio 2016, which we lost on mistakes. That's where it was clear to me that the saying, *"You don't win finals, you can only lose them,"* had some truth in it. Every goal the Argentinian made was a mistake on our part. During a game, you cannot dwell on a mistake—not for a second—because before you know it, a new situation occurs where you have to make the right decision.

When you're still dwelling on that one mistake, the next one is right around the corner. And then you are in big- time troubles. It's like in a relationship. When you dwell on a breakup, you are blind to all the other possibilities that are in front of your face. When you keep looking down, you won't see any of them. It's sad because I was like this in some parts of my life. I played a lot of international tournaments, and my performances weren't always what they are now, or the team wasn't always that good. And then you get down, because you are doing the best you can with what you have, but every time, it is not good enough. And then there are all those clichés. For example, "Belgium has a lot of unsuccessful talents;" "We aren't able to perform as a team."

You look at yourself in the mirror, and the only thing you see is a loser. You have a meeting with your coach, and he says your performance was shit. You go home, and you are smaller than the mice running around in the garbage. You think shit things. You feel shit things. You are deep. But then, out of the dark, there is a feeling of hope! You go back to a training. You meet some people, like your family and friends, and suddenly, life seems that bit much brighter. You see a good movie. The other day, I saw the Incredibles 2, in the Kinepolis. I went and saw it with my brother, Sander. I love going to cinemas. Anyway, it's an animation film, but I love those movies. It was so funny that I almost cried from laughing. I love those moments with my brother. I have the same moments with my dad, at the cinema. It makes you dream of how it could be if everyone would just be loyal to his script. I love the hidden messages in a movie, the things you don't immediately see. If you're awake, alive, and focused, you can actually learn a lot by watching movies, even the science fiction movies.

Downtime

Train, eat, sleep, and repeat. When you train, it's a challenge. You are in pain. You overcome problems. You feel you become better, stronger, and faster. But then, when you come home and have to wait till the next game, your muscles are hurting. Your soul is tired of the negativity and frustration of some of your teammates; or you are frustrated with yourself that this is everything you've got. It's just you and your thoughts, and those thoughts and feelings, like fear and doubt, take over. Is this the life I need to lead? Is this taking me somewhere? Is it worth it? Shouldn't I just go to school again? Or do I have to look for things I love and that I am passionate about, and search for my destination in this way?

Like I said, I like to follow preachers, like ET the hip-hop preacher, Jentezen Franklin, Les Brown, and John Gray, and entrepreneurs, like Gary Vee, and Edmylett. They inspire me and give me energy when I'm down. My books, and the book I'm writing, are wonderful blessings that help me through these lonely downtimes. They make me feel less alone. I naturally need people around me; so, when I'm alone, I feel sick. I got interested in Jesus. Once, my dad had an invitation for a book presentation, at the book fair in Antwerp. I almost never go to book fairs, but I have a natural interest for new things and subjects. The book presentation was about the impact of digital transformation. The impact it will have on our society etc. Very interesting. Jobs will get lost. People will have to find new things to do. As they always do. As I walked through the bookshop I was pulled towards a section. I was drifting around and came into the section where there were books of consciousness, faith, religion, Jesus etc... Very funny as these books, wh78en I started reading them, immediately caught my interest and were like oxygen to my brain. I thought it was a big miracle and saw it as a higher force saving my ass by sending me to some consciousness section saying, "Stocki, you should start reading!" I also never had the drive and discipline to actually read the books I bought, until I realised that there is a choice in life, or you learn it the hard way. And you get some scars, which will heal, but they still will be there. Or you learn every day.

You set your intention that you will learn to be able to grow. I noticed that when you truly learn, especially in the beginning, and you are conscious of the idea of transforming yourself, you'll have to go through some pain. You will end up with situations and feelings you had from the past, or traumas or decisions, which will come back to life without you even knowing it, and then you have the choice to fight or take flight. Are you willing to face them, or are you running? You'll run the rest of your life. Are you willing to open up and have the courage to go beyond pain, and go for the reward?

When you do get through it—when you do the hard stuff—life will get easy. Life will be magical! Do the hard stuff. Downtime is necessary to grow. Be careful what you do in the downtime, because addictions are formed in the dark, and they usually stay in the dark, like watching porn. At a very young age, I came in contact with porn. I think I was 14 years old, and a friend of mine was searching the internet and then came to a porn site. You don't know what you are going to see. You are stressing and looking around to make sure no one is coming, because it was clear that these sites were something you weren't supposed to see. It was amazing. The first time I saw it, it blew me away. Then, when I got older, I started looking more and more at these sites—not for hours and hours, but sometimes, especially during tournaments, you were more eager to watch it. Everyone was doing it. It was something that every friend was doing. It became so normal that you weren't cool, or something was wrong with you, if you weren't doing it...

Then my parents saw that someone visited porn sites, and that was pretty embarrassing. These were the embarrassing moments you wish you never had when you were young. But hell, I was young. That's my excuse. I quickly sensed the addicting feeling. Every time I masturbated, I had to search and see porn. Usually, I watch Passion HD, which was pretty soft. But you could easily see the other types of porn, where some of the women aren't really treated with respect, and then you wonder if this is something you should be doing.

But these things all stopped some years ago. It just stopped. It's as though it's all part of something, like I'm becoming who I'm truly meant to be. I'm working more and more on myself; I'm focused on myself. I also watched a TED Talk, by Ran Gavrieli, called *Why I Stopped Watching Porn*. I think it's really something a lot of men don't talk about, but a lot of men do it. Or boys. I did it. In general, we are vulnerable to addiction. It can bring anger and violence into your private fantasies. In visiting those sites, I also made it more possible for the industry to prevail. *"Only by watching porn do I take part in creating a demand for filmed prostitution,"* Ran Gavrieli says. He continues that *"porn promotes male dominance over women. Things which can be very disturbing and can have big influences on how you see the world and how you act in it. We are very vulnerable."*

As an athlete, you cannot eat junk. I need to eat healthy. The same goes for my mind. When I watch or see junk, my mind, which is still (!) the most powerful computer in the world, will carry the consequences; just like I can't train at the highest level when I eat junk, or play a tournament and drink beer after every game. It increases the chance of injury immensely. A teammate of mine got a serious knee injury, and he was more than six months out. The correlation between him going out that week, and his body being more tired than usual, is open for interpretation. But I've seen it happen before. So I have to feed my mind with healthy thoughts and images. No junk. I could see the difference in my life when I stopped watching porn—not that I watched it every night, especially since I have had a girlfriend for a couple of years now. But when I was younger, during puberty, as a boy, you have those moments when you are more vulnerable to porn. When you have exams and are more alone in your room; when you are in a tournament, and you're missing your girlfriend for a long time—these are moments where you are weak. Just as you have those moments where you end up eating the whole chocolate bar, or when you are scrolling the Instagram feed for two hours on the toilet, you just have those little moments in life where you are vulnerable. At least I'll say I have them. I don't have the right to speak for you.

One of the benefits, when I banned porn for good out of my life, is that I have more imagination, for example. I have more ideas and more energy. This came back in every part of my life. Watching porn once a week can have a huge impact on your mind. Ninety percent of 12- year-olds watch porn on a regular basis. It has an addictive effect, and also a paralyzing effect. In porn, you are solely judged as a man, whether you have a large penis or an eternal erection, so boys become paralyzed by these standards, and they become more aggressive. When you realise that when you're young, you are more vulnerable to role models, and you want to mirror people, you sometimes wrongly admire them.

There are examples of girls who agree to make an intimate video with a guy she has feelings for, because she wants to please him. And this guy misuses her trust, and posts it on social media. They have to leave school, they get clinically depressed and, in the worst case, they commit suicide. Or girls in commercials, like Miley Cyrus: "Girls get these notions that if you want to be worthy of love, first and foremost, you have to be worthy of sexual desire. And now, the definition of sexual desire almost equals to being like a porn star." It can get very bad.

So, I stopped. And by stopping watching porn, I chose my personal wellbeing, my intimate communication, my private erotic life, and my reclaiming of control and responsibility over my mind. And I chose to not contribute to this horrific sex industry. Where there is demand, there is supply. There is a correlation there; for example, people trafficking Asian people because there is a demand for Asian porn. This is not right. Imagine if it involved a family member. *"And I want to promote physically and emotionally safe sex. We need to put genderial hierarchy aside, subordinance aside, and bring back laughter,"* Ran Gavrieli continues. I was so impressed by his talk, it woke me up. It made me aware, even when I had already stopped watching porn. It gave me fire to join the fight and raise awareness around porn and how it affects your mind, body, and soul. One guy can make a difference. Therefore, I want to thank Ran Gavrieli for opening up and having the courage to share his story. And of course, TED, for creating this extraordinary platform of speakers who have a great impact.

Your PROBLEM is your GIFT.

Your problem is your gift. Your problem is that you think you shouldn't have any. Every problem is a present you need to unpack. Lots of times, you encounter a problem. And we live in that problem for a long time, not realising it is exactly what we need to grow. Often, confronting a problem is hurtful. It's not nice. So, we avoid it. But it sometimes takes one conversation with someone who can help you, or who went through the same problem. It is that one brief moment where someone asks you if everything is alright, and you are afraid to tell them that there are actually a lot of things that aren't alright. It's looking in the mirror and taking full responsibility of your life. Be hungry to solve the problems you face when no one believes in you, and when everyone says that it isn't possible. But know that others can help you. That's where the opportunities lie. And solving your own problem can help you help people who face the same problem. Life is great.

Habits

Complaining – battlefield instead of playfield – judging, dreaming, chatting – passive – frustration.

To be absolutely clear, these are all habits, and you can change them. You can have habits that change your life, but it starts with mindset. Your mind affects your emotions; your emotions affect your actions; your actions determine your attitude. And that all influences the quality of my life and my game. When I'm conscious that I can control all these things, I understand, more and more, that these things are the things I need to overcome.

Of course, I learned a lot already from coaches, and these subjects are brought up in preparation. But what I mostly did when I was young was to go through the motions, and wander around and then hope for the best, floating on my God-given talents. But I took leaps in my game when I started changing my habits off the field and on the field. I started to find things that worked—what I focus on, grows. So, when I focus on the referee, the referee will then be the subject after the game, and why we lost the game. I'll have the opportunity to observe myself, and to look for what went well and what can improve. But changing habits is hard. Go and try to convince someone that they complain, or that they are frustrated on the pitch, all the time, with themselves, and even worse, with others. I hear it all the time: "You won't change me." I don't want change; I want transformation and to be enlightened.

Know that paradigms are preventing you from a full and rich life. One of the biggest examples of change, and how people think, was with Copernicus. Imagine you think that the sun moves around the earth, and then, suddenly, a guy says out of nowhere that the sun is the center, and the earth moves around the sun. Every single person laughs in your face, but you know you're right, and they just don't have the curiosity and the acceptance level required to grow and expand their mind.

For concentration, I'm also reading. Since January, I've read more books in six months than I did in my entire life. There is a hunger in me. I love it. I just want to read and learn. So, I'm reading *Mindset*, by Jacki Reardon and Hans Dekker. To cut it short, it says that as an athlete, you have a *storytelling* brain, and an *action thinking* brain. The six pillars of action thinking are friendly eyes, good mistakes, curiosity, self-knowledge, self-discipline (this is my favorite), and acceptance.

Self-discipline is my favorite because this is something where you can really excel. When I decided to study at home individually, and not at school, it was because I let the circumstances overcome me, but I quickly hit a wall. I was completely relying on my self-discipline, where in the past, I used to have teachers, structure, external motivation, and peer pressure. I now had just me and my will to accomplish what I wanted or needed to accomplish. When I did nothing, nothing happened.

In sports, you cannot hide your weaknesses on the field. You can, in a way, hide yourself from the play, just by being passive or playing very simple, and not trying anything. Your weaknesses are there for everyone to see and to judge. The only thing that makes it so sweet is that with self-discipline and hard work, you can surprise everyone in an instance. You can hit the gym twice as hard. You can study. You can invest in your relationship with your teammates. Be interested instead of interesting. Have a conversation with your coach or trainer, and ask, "How do you think I'm doing? What are some of the areas I can grow in? Am I playing on my strengths?" It's sometimes hard to see what your impact is because, once you are fully focused on what you are doing, you have a blind spot— something you can't see. Once I feel in the flow, I think that's just normal for me, because then I feel good. But after training or a game, someone else would say that they were impressed, and they would get energy from me, not that I realise I'm doing so at that moment. In that moment of inspiration, I'm living in the now, in the moment, in my flow, and I'm just playing without really thinking. It's the best feeling.

For me, the morning is sometimes the hardest. When I've had a hard training the night before, I feel wrecked, like I have a hangover. Everything hurts. My head is heavy. My thoughts are quite depressing. I'm asking myself why I'm doing this, and what the point is of all this training and going through all of the hard stuff. Because of the adrenaline of the late night training, it's hard to fall asleep. I use the app, Calm, or Headspace, to fall asleep. Some meditation helps. In the morning, it's also really helpful to install some habits to get going. My mind is sometimes hard to overcome. But when I overcome it, and I set my mind straight, it's the best thing.

When you snooze, you lose. You need to win the morning back. A normal thing to do is to hit snooze and start scrolling on your Instagram, and meanwhile, thinking about all the stuff you need to do, you start stressing. You have to meet that lawyer, or answer those emails; or you have to have breakfast and take a shower. You have to call that client, go to that meeting, and clean up the house. All this stuff comes back in your head. Ninety-one percent of your thoughts are exactly the same as the day before. So sometimes it just feels like the days just keep on going, and it can make you feel depressed, worried, or anxious. The more you think about your problems and worries, the more you seem to attract them.

The best mornings are when I have a plan for getting up: I am drinking a liter of water. Because your body hasn't had anything for a whole night, while maybe you have been sweating a lot, drinking water gives your body the fluids it needs to begin the day. I do stretching, etc. (You can read the habits in the chapter called Habits), or I go to the gym. I have a good breakfast or a smoothie. I also do some reading. I read the book, *The Power of Positive Thinking*, by Norman Vincent Peale, which is great to clear the fog in your head, along with having a coffee, and writing in your journal or writing a book. Lately, I've been doing yoga in Amsterdam, and it really helps my balance and flexibility. Also, it helps me to have a clear mind and to concentrate.

A lack of focus is a dream killer. In *Mindset*, by Jackie Reardon and Hans Dekker, they talk about concentration. It's easy to wonder about many things when you are on the pitch. Yoga is also a place where I notice concentration is a big part of doing well at it: being conscious of your body, your breath, and your posture; feeling your muscles stretch; feeling the sweat on your back; feeling pain; and going out of your comfort zone. A lot of guys give up when they are tired. They give up when they are being pushed out of their comfort zone. I concentrate throughout the session, working really hard and putting myself into difficult positions, while attaining peace of mind. I put the energy where it's needed, making a conscious decision to move and keep my body in a certain position, taking control over my body.

I'll tell you that it is the best feeling to know you are in control of yourself and are realising that every part of your energy, intelligence, movement, thoughts, and creativity are in your control. When you see the possibilities and the opportunities, when anxiety and doubts are gone, problems seem just a little lighter. Challenges are smaller, failures fade away, and you can see how it made you stronger. I can look at myself and know how many times I'm really concentrating, and how many times I'm disturbed by my phone, or a beep or a comment, or thinking about what other people think.

There is an app now, called Moment, which counts the amount of hours and minutes that I'm on my phone. Every time I open my phone, it starts counting, even if I'm just watching the time. There are days when I'm on my phone for three to four hours. Imagine if I put that time into something useful, like writing or reading, or learning a new skill.

So, action mode is the most important thing. You have to take the time. I love what Les Brown says in one of his motivational videos.

*"Motivation is the desire to achieve what you believe to be worthwhile"
And many people go through life never getting in touch with their inner
greatness, because of the lack of motivation to push themselves (Push
yourself!), or because they have not found something that they believe
to be worthwhile challenging themselves for. I heard a poem once:
Many a flower has bloomed unceasingly, and wasted sweetness upon
the cold desert air. When translated, it means that many talented
persons have gone unnoticed, and the world never had a chance to be
exposed to their talent, because that person did not take the time to
begin to express, or to demonstrate or to motivate, themselves in the
direction to bring that which they came into the universe to bring.*

*How can you measure your motivation? How can you evaluate where
you are on a scale of one to ten? Let's do this for ourselves mentally.
How do you rate yourself, from one to ten, regarding your mental
attitude, how you feel about yourself, and how you feel about life? How
do you rate yourself, on a scale of one to ten, in terms of your physical
appearance, or in terms of your health? Do you take care of yourself?
Are you allowing yourself to get overweight and out of shape? Are you
watching the food that you put into your body? Are you conscious of
your health? Do you make a deliberate effort to exercise?*

*It was George Burns who said, "We cannot help getting older, but we
don't have to get old." And many of us get old before our time, because
we don't take time to take care of ourselves. Your environment is a very
good indicator. On a scale of one to ten, is it what you want it to be?
Do you find it desirable? Are you satisfied with the job or career that
you're involved in? Someone said that 85% of the American public are
unhappy with their jobs. Are you spending eight hours a day just
spending time doing something that you don't find challenging, and
which does not make you stretch mentally, and does not stimulate or
inspire you? Is it something that you don't find a sense of fulfilment in?*

*If you are doing that day in and day out, it has to affect how you feel
about yourself, your level of motivation, and your relationships. What*

kind of impact is it having on your life? Is it nourishing, or is it a toxic relationship? Does it drain you or does it build you up? Ask yourself that. How motivated are you to do something about it? What is your contribution, your actions? What are you giving? Many people will leave the universe without a trace. No one will know they were here. And in fact, under their name, we can put "not used up." Will anybody know that you came this way? What contribution are you giving? What will you leave? What will be different because you came this way? Someone once told me that life is our gift that God has given us, and how we live our lives is our gift to God. What kind of gift are you formulating?

I don't care who you are or what you do… Sometime you are going to get tired. And sometime you are going to get in a rut. Sometimes it will seem like nothing you do works out right. And sometimes it will seem like you don't have the will to do anything. Sometimes it will seem like you're punch drunk, fading through life, day in and day out, looking at non-discriminatory television—anything that's on—just looking. And you'll feel depressed, powerless, useless, and bored. What do you do? How do you get yourself out of that rut, when you know you can do more than what you have been doing, and you are not doing it? When you are discontented with where you are, and you get angry at yourself? How do you get out of that rut? How do you motivate yourself?

One of the things that we must do is that we must be involved and working on achieving self-mastery. You must work on yourself continuously. Never be satisfied with yourself. Investing the effort and time on yourself is the greatest ability that human beings have above animals. A dog can't be anything but a dog; a tree can't be anything but a tree, but human beings have unlimited potential. You can put effort into yourself, and by concentrating on yourself, and developing yourself, you can transform your life, wherever you are right now.

So you want to work on yourself. You want to read books that inspire you and motivate you. You want to listen to tapes, over and over and over again. And I suggest that you listen to tapes when you first get up in the morning. You want to control the spirit of your day. When you first wake up in the morning, your mind is operating on 10.5 wave cycles per second. That's when the subconscious mind is most impressionable. Whatever you hear in the first twenty minutes when you wake up, that's what's going to affect the spirit of your day. When you listen to tapes, listen with relaxed belief, believing that this could happen for you. And by listening to them over and over and over again, you will get a breakthrough.

You can listen to the same tapes for months, and all of a sudden, you will hear something you never heard before, and it will have a special meaning for you. Or if you read the same book, you'll find some special insight. You'd say that you can't believe you didn't see that the first time. So you want to be involved in developing yourself. Most people won't do that. Most people take that kind of effort, and invest that kind of energy in themselves, but they will fall prey to that conversation within: "Oh, don't do that; you don't have time; you're too busy; you're too caught up in the rat race." Most people won't do that. They won't take time to go to lectures. They won't take time to go to seminars. They won't take time to go to classes to improve themselves. And as you begin to continue to work on yourself, you will begin to expand your vision of yourself. You will begin to work towards self-mastery. And you will begin to see that it reflects itself on all the dimensions of your life: your mental life, your physical life, your social life, your monetary life, and in your relations.

So, concentrate on developing yourself because, if you don't, you will begin to make a settlement. Most people already have. What kind of settlement have you made with your life? You know you can make out of court settlements. Have you ever heard of them? That means that you decided to take something less than what you originally wanted to get, had you gone into court. And the reason that you settle outside of court is because you didn't believe that you could get it. So you made an out of court settlement. Many of us are making an in life settlement. We are settling for less than what we actually deserve. We don't feel good about it, but we make it work inside of our minds. We'll come up with some kind of excuse to make it alright.

What kind of settlement have you made with your life? Many of us settle for less than what we want out of relationships because we don't have the courage to change them. I had a seminar I used to do: Are you living together or dying together? Many people are just dying together! We used to have a song that said, "Neither one of us wants to be the first to say goodbye."

The next thing is to find some keys to self-motivation, to drive yourself in addition to working on yourself. As you work on yourself, you feel good about yourself, and as you feel better about yourself, you treat yourself differently. Develop a health plan. You can't feel well and do well if you don't have good health. You can't perform if you don't have good health. Your health is valuable. Develop a health plan, a plan that you will follow, because this is the vehicle that has to carry you through this experience called life. You want to take good care of it because you love yourself enough, and you care enough about yourself. And that's not easy.

It is not easy having a health plan and sticking to it, but you're worth it, and worth doing it again and again and again. I have lost twenty-two pounds several times. I always do it. I love potato chips. People who know me, know that I also love M&M peanuts. I love peanut butter and jelly sandwiches. I love my mother's sweet potato pie; it's not always on my health plan, but I put it on there sometimes. I say life is too short to go without sweet potato pie.

The next key thing, as you take care of yourself, is self-motivation. You want to live life with energy and passion. You want to make a conscious effort to be lively. You see, in life, you either say hello or goodbye. You are either on the way or in the way. Leave those people alone. Some folks are just walking around looking and saying, "How are you doing honey?" Stay away from those people. Just stay away from them. It affects you. You want to smile. You want to be happy. You have a lot to be thankful for. But you watch some of the faces around you, and I tell you, some of these faces, they will put you in a depressed state of mind. So you want to avoid these kinds of faces. When you see them coming, turn your head.

The next thing is that you want to monitor your inner conversations, the things that you say to yourself. You want to watch them, and by watching them, you want to take charge. A friend of mine told me— and she did it excellently—"I didn't want to come tonight. I was feeling so depressed, but I said I'm going anyhow." See, that was the conversation: "Oh, you really don't feel like it. You really don't need to do it. You don't need to read anything." Forget all that. That's that inner conversation. "Oh, you don't need to worry about trying to go into your own business. Forget that; you can't do that. What if you lose everything you have?"

That inner conversation that stops you from doing the thing you want to do? Don't do that. "How can you possibly think about being a motivational speaker? You don't have the context; you don't have the money. You don't know the right people. You are going to get up there, and your mind is going to go blank. Forget all that. You remember that time you got up before some people, and you panicked? You stood up, and your mind sat down? Don't you remember?" And I said, "Yes," and then I said, "Shut up!" So you have got to learn to stand up for yourself, inside yourself. Short circuit and override that conversation that's always going on. Eighty-five percent of what that conversation will tell you is negative. It will tell you you're tired when you really are not tired. It will tell you that you can't do it; it will fill you with fear. So you have to watch that conversation, and when you find it going on, you have to stand up and say, "I'm going to do this anyhow. I'm afraid, *but I'm afraid not to do it. And I'm not going to let you stop me."*

The biggest challenge that you will have in life is you. There is an old African proverb that says, "When there is no enemy within, the enemy outside can do us no harm." The next thing that is key to self-motivation is that you have to ask yourself, "What do I want out of life?" What do you want out of life? What do you want out of a job? What do you want out of a career? What do you want out of a relationship? What do you want? What gives you your life? How will you know when you have it? What will make you happy?

You need to know. You need to start asking yourself some questions. What do I really, truly want? And you need to be exact about that. Don't be vague: "Oh, I just want to be happy." That's too vague. What will make you happy? How will you know when you have it? Zero in on it. Be exact. Be specific. And as you do that, it will stimulate that superconscious mind, or the Reticular Activating system of your mind, which will begin to find those things to identify with it. And once you begin to determine what you want, take the time to write it down. Don't just think about it. Write it down. That is the subjective process that engages the subconscious mind. Write it down. Once you write it down, read it three times a day—morning, noon, and night.

Why is that important? Because it will cause you to focus. It will cause you to concentrate. When that other conversation is going on, telling you what you cannot do, and telling you all of the impossibilities and all of the obstacles, your concentrating will begin to create a larger vision within yourself, and you'll start looking for and seeing some new opportunities. You start creating some openings for yourself. As you begin to read that every day, day in and day out, that will make you focus! That will discipline your thinking. And you'll get all kinds of creative ideas.

As I talk to you right now, being involved in this immersion process, you are going to create some openings for yourself. You are going to get some ideas. You are going to feel the adrenaline flowing, and you are going to think about something, some idea you had. And you'll say, "I want to go back, and I'm going to look at that again from a different vantage point, not from the level of the problem or the obstacles that I encountered, but from a higher vantage point." What you will begin to see and to know, as I talk to the higher consciousness within you, is that you are powerful, and you are a miracle worker. That inner conversation has conditioned you to believe that you are not. As you begin to discover the truth of who you are—no matter what challenge you are facing in life (and if you're living, you are facing some challenge)—you begin to know that you are powerful and that you are a miracle maker.

So, as you begin to write down exactly what it is that you want, read it every day. The next thing is to see yourself there. How will you feel once you get there? What will the experience be like for you? What will be different? What kind of person do you have to become in order to get there? Visualize yourself there, living the experience. I remember when I ran for state representative in Columbus, Ohio. I had a lot of people telling me (You have to watch not only the conversation within but the conversation without.), "Les, you can't possibly win. You can't do that."

I went down to the legislature, and I saw myself. I knew what I wanted. I saw myself in the chair. I pointed out the chair that I wanted. I used to go and sit up in the galleries and watch the legislated process. I used to go to the committee meetings and listen to legislation being introduced. I learned how to write legislation, and how to amend legislation. I started thinking like a legislator. I got up every day, dressing and thinking like that, and selling myself on it. I was seeing myself as the legislator: "Mister Speaker, this is the gentleman from the 29th house... I went into the legislature; I walked right on. I had the experience of it. And when I ran and won against overwhelming odds, they were shocked. I won the election even before it was held, because I was living it in my mind.

You want to see yourself beyond your circumstances. If you have a challenge, see yourself beyond your challenge. See yourself with the challenge already resolved, and knowing that all is well. See yourself in control and in charge of your destiny, being healthy and happy. The next important thing in the area of motivating yourself is to know why you are doing it. Your mind will say, "Why bother? Why go through all this? This is too hard. No; throw in the towel. It's not worth it."

Has it ever said that to you before? Here is how you can handle that and override that. Write down five reasons why you deserve it. Why do you deserve what you want? Why you? Why do you deserve it? What meaning and value will it bring to your life? What is so different about you that you deserve your goal? When you have those five reasons written down, and when you have some down moments (and you are going to have them) when that conversation starts talking to you (and it's going to talk to you), you can pull that out and read it, and it will build you up. It will be your rod and staff to comfort you through some challenging moments, because you are going to have some.

Life will knock you between the eyes. It will catch you on the blind side and come out of nowhere with stuff you can't anticipate. It will knock the wind out of you. You'll want to give up. That's why it is important to work on yourself: listening to tapes; building yourself up; and talking to yourself, with power, feeling, and conviction. Build yourself up, day in and day out, because it's coming—I guarantee you. Life is just waiting: "Oh, he's doing well now, huh? Very good." I remember when I had an experience. I was pursuing my dream, and that's why you have to work on yourself. You don't know what is going to happen.

When you are working on a larger vision, you have to really work on yourself, because life will catch you on the blind side. You better be ready. You better make sure you want it, because it will make you cry. Life will wear you out. You'll be saying, "No, I can't," and "No, I won't." You will be trying to read, but you won't be able to see anything through the tears.

The next thing is, whatever you do, you want to develop technical mastery. You want to be the best in what you do. You want to master it. Part of self-motivation is that you have to find something that gives you a strong sense of competence— where you become known for that. You develop a reputation of being good at doing that. You set some high personal standards for yourself. You are not competing with anybody else. You are just unfolding yourself to be the best person that you can be. You want to give the best quality service that you can give, because that is a statement about who you are.

The other thing that's key to self-motivation is to recognise the fact that you are going to get into some slumps. Recognise the fact that you are going to encounter a great deal of failure in life. It goes with the territory. But in the face of that, you want to be relentless. When you want something, don't expect everybody to say, "Oh, come on in; do you want this? Oh, great, we want to give this to you. You're such a nice person. You are doing it for your family, aren't you? Great." No, no; life isn't like that. Many doors will be closed in your face. There will be many loans that you will want, and they'll say no. "You don't have enough collateral. You don't have enough credit." And most people will give up. But you have got to decide that you're going to be fearless: Refuse to be denied; go all out; be relentless, and don't care how many no's you encounter.

I like something Eric Thomas says when he's getting ready for a basketball game. He says, "I'm going to either shoot us in or shoot us out. But I'm not going to not do anything." And that's the way to go. You can't make a basket unless you shoot the ball. You can't hit a homerun unless you take a swing at it. Most people won't even take a swing. "Well, I probably won't make it anyhow." That's the conversation within. "They probably won't give it to me anyhow." If you want something, you have to be relentless. You have to decide: "I deserve this, and I'm going to have it." And you go all out to get it. That drives it. The next thing is, when you want something out of life, you have to be willing to go into action. Don't wait around for things to be just right. Don't wait for things to be perfect. Don't wait for the ideal situation, because it will never be ideal. There will always be a reason: "Well, as soon as the children grow up," or, "As soon as I pay my bills," or, "As soon as I get my divorce," or, "As soon as I get enough money together."

There are all kinds of excuses. Do what you can, where you are, with what you have. And never be satisfied. A lot of people never take a chance in life. They don't want to take any chances. They want the situation to be ideal. That's not walking by faith; that's walking by sight. "If I can see it, I'll do it." No, no, no. A lot of people say, "If I can see it, I believe it." No, no, no. If you believe it, you can see it. And don't be disturbed when no one else can see it. That's not unusual. That is ordinary. But because you want some different kind of results in your life, you have to be willing to be unreasonable.

If you want unreasonable results in your life, you have to be willing to be unreasonable. Part of being unreasonable is that you don't judge according to appearances. Part of being unreasonable is that "you can see it because you believe it." That's part of being unreasonable. Part of being unreasonable is like Paul, who said, "You must have the faith to call forth those things that be not as though they were." That's part of being unreasonable. Most people won't do that. Most people say, "Call me when you get it together. Then I'll support you."

The other thing that is key to self-motivation, which empowers you, is that you want to find a cause larger than yourself. Find something that you can contribute to. Find something where you can make a difference, because you can. It is part of what feeds your larger vision, and part of what gives you a reason for being; and part of what gives you your life is by giving something back. Then you'll say, "Well, I can't afford to give anything." You can't afford not to give. Give your time. Give your talent. It is nothing to just go around and lick envelopes. "I don't know exactly what I'm going to do, but I'm going over there." It's part of my tiding in the universe.

Once you develop that special sense of mission—and that's what you develop when you are part of a larger cause than yourself—it drives you. You don't need an alarm clock to get up in the morning. You have special power. You go places, and folks like to be around you. They will know there is something different about you. When you go in, they'll say, "Hey, that's somebody important; I want to know who they are. I just want to be near them and that energy that they have." That consciousness that you embody will affect everybody around you.

The next thing is that you want to create a home court advantage for yourself. You have to be aware of who you have around you. So you want to be selective. Have friends that will enable you to grow. I have friends that enable me to grow spiritually. These are my spiritual friends. I talk spiritual stuff with them. I have some other friends that are intellectual friends. They make me grow intellectually. They make me stretch. I have some professional friends. I get together with other professional speakers, and we learn from each other. We grow from each other. I have other friends who are just social friends. All we do is socialise together—nothing heavy up in here.

The relationships that you develop can enhance and enrich your life, or they can drain you. I know many talented people who had a great deal of potential, but because they didn't surround themselves with other people that would inspire them to transcend themselves, they never realised their greatness, and they will end up going to their grave with all their good stuff still in them. So you want to look at your relationships: the people that you are involved with, and the people that you communicate with most often. You want to ask yourself the questions: "What am I becoming because of this relationship? Does it inspire me? Am I motivated? Am I encouraged? Am I driven to develop myself? Am I seeking my own greatness? What kind of person am I becoming because of this relationship? Am I becoming more cynical and negative about life?" Ask yourself that.

The next thing is that you have to say yes to your life. You have to say, "YES!!" Yes, to my dreams; yes, to me; yes, I can make it; yes, I can—it doesn't matter how many failures I have had; it doesn't matter how many mistakes I have endured; it doesn't matter about my defeats; it doesn't matter about what I have done. "YES! YES!" I don't care about the fact I'm in a hole now. It doesn't matter about where I am. "YES!" The last chapter of my life has not been written yet. If you judge me now, you judge me prematurely. I haven't exposed all my stuff yet. I'm still in the process of transforming my life. I'm still in the process of becoming. "YES!" I had somebody in my life once who told me that I'd never make it. And I said, "I'll show you." And what energized me and what motivated me was something Frank Sinatra said: "The best revenge is massive success." I'll show you! You just watch my smoke. So, say, "YES!"

Stand up for your dreams. Decide that you are going to stand up for your life. Decide that your life is so meaningful to you and that you love yourself, and you love life so much that you are going to stand up for something you want. Stand up for what you believe in, because you could fall for anything. You are powerful. You have miracle powers working in your life right now. But you have to work on yourself—you have to develop yourself; you have to talk to yourself—day in and day out, selling yourself and your potential. And you have to know that you are worth all of your effort, and that the key to your motivation, as you get a larger vision of yourself, is to know that you have something to give, and that you have a reason to be here in the universe at this point in time. I want you to stand up for your life. Stand up for your dream!"
– Les brown.

I love Les Brown and what he stands for. I am sure that when more people hear his message, they will live a more fulfilling and better life. They will find their greatness and light up this world more. There is no darkness; darkness is just the absence of light.

Have Some PASSION!
Don't just go around and get through the day! Be grateful! Be happy towards the people you encounter. Encourage them. Ask them about their goals and dreams, and maybe there is the possibility that you can help them achieve theirs. Maybe, someday, they will help you achieve yours! Be grateful you have a roof over your head, and that you have people who you love and they love you. Be grateful you can read books, eat, sleep, be warm, and go travelling.

Stop PROCRASTINATING
Stop SABOTAGING yourself.

Stop BLAMING other people!
Stop looking for the right person. BE the right person.

Chapter 7

Fighting for What I Want

Overcoming Challenges

Life happens for you, not to you.

Sometimes I feel sad. It's as if I'm not trusting my teammates that they are doing the right things. They act out of fear. My challenge is that I don't dwell on what others do and lose my own focus. The only thing I can control is myself. That's the starting point. By changing myself, others will follow. At least that's my call. I can only give the right example. And from that, I can help others. As Patrick Lencioni so wonderfully explains in one of his books, the five frustrations of teamwork are: lack of trust (the number one frustration), fear of conflicts, lack of commitment, avoidance of accountability, and inattention to results.

The challenge I face now is that I can see these things everywhere I go, so I have to be careful that I'm not overdoing it. But then again, I struggle with the fact that maybe it's my responsibility to put those things out there. The other day, we had a teambuilding, where half of the team went out really late. The next day, we had a practice game, and as it was a teambuilding weekend, it was permitted to go out as a team. Some believe strongly in having a good night out together and then bearing the consequences together as a team, and showing your mental strength by playing the game and working hard for your team. I get that. During the game, you could clearly see that the hard work was there, but the quality was poor. Still, I found it heartwarming to see the team working hard for each other under those circumstances.

But then the week began, and half of the team was sick in bed with diarrhea and throwing up, as a result of the heavy weekend with three games and a heavy night out. I almost tore my hamstring again. Then I asked myself if it was worth it. Even when guys drink twenty beers, they still can't find a way to communicate about the things that matter. I never feel good in these moments. I can feel the strength in team sports, and I can get really excited about it.

Nic Wilson, a writer who wrote well over a hundred books, wrote a book about superconsciousness and the ability of humans to experience peak experience. I still have to finish it. Being superconscious is something that intrigues me, and something I want to learn more about: to get more out of life; to be able to stretch myself more mentally; to search for something more, something within me, something deeper. I can feel it so strongly sometimes that I almost start crying. It is a feeling of intense emotion when a team has the right mindset, are living for their dream, their goal, and for each other, and are willing to go the extra mile, realising that when a team plays as it should—when the *hum* starts—it is better to watch a game than go to the doctor, not merely seeing it as a side thing but seeing the game as the one thing to strive for.

It is the one thing you put all your energy into and focus on. You inspire people. You give them an unforgettable experience. You take them on a journey, where there are all the elements of life. You start equal, but you get behind. You need to work harder to get back. The other team controls your plays. They know what you are going to do, but you find a way to win. You are creative, and you show tremendous willpower. You realise that when you focus on one thing, everything else will fall into place. The universe will help you when you have the right heart behind your goals. You will not have to force anything, but everything will fall into place. People will start to help you and give their time and energy. You will attract the right people, people who support you. The energy around you will be so strong and warm that people will just want to be near you.

Imagine a house in which you're locked up, and the only way out is one door. In order to open that door, you need to build muscles. You need to have a super-brain to break the lock. You'll need to smash the door open with all your might and everything you've got. You'll have to develop all your talents and your gifts. And when you reach your full potential, then, and only then, you are permitted to go through the door. Will you be willing to do the things necessary to live a life of discipline—to starve all distractions, to grow, to develop—or are you going to crumble on the sofa, watching Netflix series, eating Cheetos, scrolling through social media, playing games, and throwing time in the garbage? You wouldn't be using the talents you have, like dancing and singing, putting joy in the hearts of people, and being of service to a cause larger than yourself. That's where life sometimes has me, because to be able to develop those talents, you have to go through pain and sacrifices. People will hurt you and lie to you. Changing your life isn't easy. It's hard. There will be times you want to quit, and throw the towel in the ring.

Olympics

Suddenly, I was there, in the Olympic Village, surrounded by athletes from all around the world. I remember when I was young, my father, at the table in the morning, asked everyone what they dreamed about. And so he came to me, and I just remembered a vague dream about the world. I remembered I could see the world, and he would laugh because I said, *"...the world, Dad."* I never got why that was so weird. But here I was in the Olympic village, surrounded by people from all over the world. It was magical. I was on my bike at night as I saw all these different nationalities together with all their own personalised suits. It was beautiful: the world in one place, with all these athletes, and the best of their country about to inspire their nation, families, friends, and the world.

Only a few would reach the absolute top. Would I be one of them, I wondered? My whole life came together. I had quit school, went full on hockey, and was physically at the top of my ability. I knew the tactics, and I was mentally confident in my abilities and skills. Now was the moment to shine, and it was a very special feeling. I enjoyed it. Trainings were done. It was like when you go to an exam and you know that you are prepared in the best way possible. I was not stressed. It was one of the most wonderful moments of my life. I had a strong feeling of me deserving to be there, to be a part of the Olympics. Once a dream, it was now a reality. But a reality I had influence on.

I still had to make it happen. It hit me that the one thing driving the Olympics was people. It's people: individuals striving for excellence, friendship, and respect—the three values of the Olympics. These values are there for us to show to the outside world. The sense of responsibility came over me. If not me, who else? And then you have the superstars: athletes who can't come into the big eating hall because when they do, everyone wants to take a picture with them—people like Usain Bolt, Michael Phelps, Raphael Nadal, or Lebron James. The eating hall is so big. Over a thousand athletes need to eat there. And they are fired up and hungry. So when one of these athletes comes in, you can hear in the distance a group of people going absolutely bonkers, screaming and running towards the person. That's why they call them superstars. They attract other stars towards them. And a new universe is made.

Team

Together, everyone achieves more. It is one cliché that you hear a lot. I think that's true for the most part. But you also need a big part of individual genius: people like Einstein, Van Gogh, Steve Jobs, Bill Gates, Picasso, Abraham Lincoln, and Jesus. All these people made the group enhance. They were willing to take the step forward when no one else would, to take the leap when no one else had the courage to do so. They were willing to make the decision and go for it. Sometimes it takes one guy on the team to make the difference. But of course, when one guy takes a leap into the abyss, it's good you don't follow a stupid leader.

Then again, there are times where you just want to stay in bed, like those cold, November mornings where you feel the cold outside your bed and just feel like staying warm inside the house. But you have to make the journey to school. The drizzling rain just makes it all that more painful. Yet when you finish that day and have done everything you had to do, you feel joy and light. You enjoy life on a bigger scale. You don't feel the rain anymore. You just get wet. You see the little things become the big things. The commitment to details makes your energy flow, and life is a wonderful thing.

When a group of people focus on the same craft, when their energy flows to one thing—in sport, it can be the ball, or your specific role on the team—the team starts flowing. Everybody is committed and ready to put their body, soul, mind, and heart on the field. They are prepared, focused, and ready to overcome every challenge presented by the other team. They have confidence in their own ability, playing the game regardless of the scoreboard, the referee, or the circumstances. Knowing that you're in control, you decide that the locus of control is you. *You* make things happen, and things like *luck* and *coincidence* disappear.

Think Like a Pro

Complaining, locus of control, no fun, stress, no creativity, traffic, bubble, hockey, real life, workshops, players going out, players not working hard in the gym, clubs that work against the national team. criticism—the level of participation equals the value you get out. Mirror. Take accountability for your actions. There are a lot of things that come to mind. From a young age, what drove me was the thought of being a pro. There was a voice in my head that said, "You can be a pro if you want to, Emmanuel. It's up to you. It's your decision." Live on purpose for what you do; be of the biggest value you can be for your team and the people around you. What does it take to be a pro? What do you need to do to become a pro? Maybe I'm far off what it could be. What is holding me back from becoming the best version of me?

Certainly, in the beginning, I was busy with what others did. I remember Marc Lammers had a report about the skills you should have as a player: running push, flick, stroke, shot, flats, backhand shot, defensive tackle, interception, and so on. On every skill, you had to give yourself a quotation. So if I had a good goal shot, I would give myself an eight out of ten, where Mark Lammers and Jeroen Delmee would say, "We think it's a six out of ten because it is still too irregular." And so it goes for every skill.

Of course, I thought of myself as a bigshot. I was playing on the national team. We would be in the news. My family was proud, and my school was proud. But then Mark would say, "Well, compare yourself now with Jamie Dwyer, four or five times the best player in the world." Then you become very small because you realise that you are nowhere near the guy. That was when I was eighteen. Never could I have imagined that I would play with him for one year in Bloemendaal in the same shirt—the guy who I had to compare myself with was now playing with me on the same pitch.

Also, it's hard because we are the average of the five people we spend the most time with. So, are the people around me trying to be better people? Are they pushing and challenging themselves? Are they stretching and improving their skillset? Or are they just wandering through life and hoping for the best? What I want to achieve for myself, by writing this book, is to find out what things I need to do in order to become the best version of myself on the pitch. And I have three months till the world cup in India. It will take everything I have in order to have a chance to win it. We need four games, minimum, to win, and to do something we have never done in the entire history of Belgium. I am willing to change myself. I am looking for habits and implementing them in my life to achieve this goal, so I can show that it's possible to achieve your dreams and goals. But it's hard.

The Borlées, The Belgian Tornados, are the European champions once again of the four times 400 metres, and they asked the father, Jacques Borlée, who is the coach, what it is that is so special about his approach. These questions always pop up when someone is successful. How did they do it? Maybe more interesting to know is why they did it, or why they do it, instead of always focusing on the "what" and the "how." Speaker and author, Simon Sinek, wrote an interesting book that states people should start with "why," instead of focusing on what the job would bring. I hear a lot of people talk about what car they would get, what house they would buy, and what fancy brands they would buy if they were earning a lot of money. I'm not saying it's bad, but start with "why" you would do what you do. Because when you know your "why," it will stir something deeper within you. You'll wake up before your alarm clock. You'll have more energy. You will be able to cope with the pressure. It will give you the edge, the advantage, and the lift that you need.

Being a professional is just something I want to achieve right now, to be of great value to the teams I play on, and to inspire others. What I love is when people or friends I hadn't seen for a very long time come to me and say that they saw a goal of mine, and they are really excited when they talk about the things I'm doing with hockey. Of course, they knew me when I was going to school with them. It gives me energy to move on and to believe more in what I'm doing. It makes all the sacrifices bearable. It makes the pain a little bit lighter.

Passion

The suffering and death of Jesus; strong and barely controllable emotion; the passion of Christ: Would you be able to suffer for several days on the cross, dying from exhaustion and asphyxiation (the state or process of being deprived of oxygen, which can lead to death)? Would you be willing to die so others could have their sins forgiven? How is it that the death of one man could achieve so much? This is the ultimate passion: the passion of Christ. He was constantly seduced by the devil to give in. He was seduced by hatred and anger. Still, he chose love.

Sometimes I have asphyxiation, when there is a lot of pressure, and I have to start playing really hard despite my exhaustion and stress, and maybe not having the most confidence. It's in my head that things have to change. When I miss a ball or a dribble, or am just not in the game, I need to get out of my head and stop saying to myself that I should've done this or that. I have to start saying that I need to get back in position, and start over.

Reboot, just like when your computer is jammed. Turn the on/off button and start over. You'll actually see that no one really cares about the mistake. They care about the attitude you have after the mistake. How good is your tackleback? How well are you defending? I go and go until I get a breakthrough at the right moment; this is usually based on intuition and the feeling I have about how the team is playing. When I'm in my flow, the ball and stick are one, and I don't have to think about it. I'm guided in a way on what to do. When I start thinking and stressing, it sometimes looks like I just can't handle the ball that well. Or it feels like that.

You have to be flexible with what the team needs at that point. Norman Vincent Peale says in his book, *Positive Thinking*, *"The person who sends out positive thoughts activates the world around him positively, and draws back to himself positive results."* When things are going bad, or when you start a game, or, like in my life, I'm about to get the ball, expect the best. *"When you expect the best, you release magnetic forces in your mind, which, by the law of attraction, tends to bring the best to you."* So, when you do something, do it with passion. Expect the best. Do it with enthusiasm. *"There is real magic in enthusiasm. It spells the difference between mediocrity and accomplishment."*– Norman Vincent Peale. *"Imagination is the true magic carpet."* I just love these words. They are music to my ears. Whenever I feel down or bad, I look these things up, and they give me energy. Passion also means pain.

Pain

You have a choice in life: either the pain of change or the pain of regret. When you start fighting for what you want, it's painful. People say, "Oh, it's so nice to do what you like." They say it now when they see me having success. But what about the times when we didn't win? Because when I lost, it was just me and my flaws, me and another failure in my life. You get what you deserve. You get out what you put in. I have troubles because when I feel like shit and think negative thoughts, I sense that this has an effect on the team. I lose the ball quicker or my actions don't work. People around me start being frustrated with me because I didn't do what they wanted me to do. And most of the time, I start dribbling and I lose vision. Isn't it the same in life?

When you are stressed and troubled, and start thinking negatively about life, your world becomes really small; you start worrying too much about your own stuff, and you take yourself too seriously. You get cynical about what you're doing. You lose perspective, and you lose connection with the people around you. Your timing is bad. Pain is everywhere. When you discipline your life, it's painful. I have a bad habit of being late. I need to work on that. When I'm late, I'll get reactions from my teammates, and then I'll be on time. But then, after a while, I am in my car, driving towards a team meeting or training, and I manage to be late, because I was doing whatever thing.

I guess, at those moments, my monkey-mind is working. And then I'm embarrassed. I'm ashamed of myself for being late. I want to work on myself, but still, these things come up. I said sorry to the team, but actions speak louder than words. But my point is, it's painful to change. I need to look in the mirror and say, "Well, I'm no good in this area of my life, and I need to work on it, because me being late impacts the team." You can't imagine how influential and powerful you can be to a team. There are, seriously, no limits. What you put in, you get out. Period. It's true. So, when you take accountability to change yourself for the better—to become healthy, wealthy, and fit, and be on time— you'll be amazed at what you're capable of if you use the pain to push yourself to greatness, and if you're able to take it in and get it to your soul.

Write everything down. I hate it when people put me on the spot when I'm late. It's painful. It messes with my pride and ego. So I write it down in big letters in my notebook, which I always carry around—in big letters, BE ON TIME—so people can start counting on me. They can see the drive I have. And don't be *on time*—be early. Be half an hour early. I created this rightback type of beast who is willing to smash brick walls to get the win. I lost myself a bit in this role for my team. But sometimes that's what it takes to achieve what you want.

In order to be successful, you must be willing to do the things today that others won't do, in order to have the things tomorrow that others won't have. Every time I go back to that gym to work on myself, to get the negative thoughts out of my head, I am saying to myself that it's possible: "It's possible; it's possible; you're the one; you're the one; you can make it happen; use the pain to push you, so you won't have the pain of regret."

Listen to MOTIVATIONAL messages in the MORNING

Listen to positive messages in the morning. Win back your morning. Be mindful of how social media influences your mind early in the morning. The first things you do in the morning impacts the rest of your day. Have a cold shower. Brush your teeth. Do a workout. Have a power smoothie. Have a smoothie with oat milk, blueberries, banana, chia seeds, grains, oatmeal flakes, and a shot of espresso, and go kick ass. Write down why you are happy today, what you are enjoying today, what you are excited about today, what it is that makes you proud today, and who it is that you love. Get your mind set for the day, and manifest greatness. Go RUN every day. It reduces stress and enhances your creativity. Read spiritual quotes in the morning. READ! Read positive books. Learn a language! Use your time.

Chapter 8

Looking for Help

Professional Help

I'm not perfect, but who is? However, I can have a perfect vision. When I was down after a tournament in India, I was devastated. Again, we couldn't make it happen for the Belgian national team. Throughout our history, it appears very difficult to have a consistent, successful team in our country. It's my mission to achieve this goal—to have a successful team, to represent a nation, and a team that inspires a nation—but it's difficult. It's hard every time you get smacked in the face. Just today, we lost 7–1 against Oranje Rood, in a practice game. And next week, the competition starts. We had a tough week behind us. We played three games in a row during the weekend in Hamburg, followed by a team night out. Then I had, on Monday, recovery/hockey training; Tuesday, double session; Wednesday, a small hockey session and recovery; Thursday, a game with two different opponents; and Friday, an extra session—only to get smacked in the face on Saturday.

I was so angry and frustrated. Sometimes it seems like you're climbing a mountain and doing everything in your power to achieve the top, but you fall down exactly where you started, which is demoralizing. It was also a long time ago. I felt so lonely and lost on the pitch. I couldn't get the energy to fight or lift the team up. Emotionally and physically, I hit a wall. I was not feeling confident, and I was not able to run the tackleback. Because I get very negative, and I can't control my thoughts, I start judging others: I start saying to myself that a certain player is playing shitty, and not stopping balls. I'm doubting if he is giving everything he has for the team. I'm thinking that he isn't wanting to invest in himself and others. Then I start thinking that I just want to stop playing and go home and start something else; that I should just quit this hockey game.

But then again, I can move on. I have confidence that I will be where I want to be, putting in the hard work, acknowledging the hard work ahead, and enjoying the process. When I am down like I am at these points, I look at myself. After judging everyone else, it comes down to judging yourself. And then, usually, I judge myself for judging, which is pretty stupid. But then, again, I notice that I live for this game, to inspire. But it doesn't show. I'm doing everything to be in the best form—at least, in my little universe, I think I'm doing the right things. But then I play so shitty. Or the team plays so shitty. And I feel so bad and ashamed for this unbelievable, disastrous performance from myself and/or the team, that I want to throw in the towel.

Sports is mentally a hard game. That's why I like to talk to professional sports psychologists. Jef Brouwers had a big part. He was the psychologist for the national team. I really loved his philosophy. He gave me such great insights, and I loved listening to his views on the game. Ellen Schouppe also helped me a lot after my breakdown in 2018, when I voluntarily didn't go to the stage of the national team, to work with Ellen. We actually just talked about everything, especially how I got here and why I now had such resentment towards the national team.

Some subjects, I got pretty emotional about. For example, when I spoke about my father for the first time, a lot of emotion came out. I think it's because we have built a strong relationship. He was always there alongside the line—seeing me play bad; seeing me play good; seeing me play great; seeing me be unstoppable; seeing me win; seeing me cry; seeing me disappointed; being sad and frustrated himself; being overly happy; seeing us grow and become stronger, faster, bigger, louder; seeing us make decisions; and seeing me suffer—having all these emotions. He always says, "Sports is life. Everything is in there: greed, selfishness, selflessness, deception, realness, emotion, character, belief, despair, doubt, winning, and losing.

My dad also had some rough periods in his career. I always like to think that my hockey games and tournaments and successes made him happier. There, I saw the overlapping areas of business and top sports; where the mentality and attitude you have is everything. The other day, I spoke to my sister, who studied psychology in Leuven. It was her birthday, and I and my father, mother, brother-in-law, and mother of my brother-in-law, were sitting in the living room. Everybody gave a short speech, starting with my dad, and then everybody followed, except the mother of my brother-in-law. Then you get that feeling that it's your turn to speak, so I did. I already felt that if I spoke, I probably would get emotional somewhere along the line. But I had to, so I started.

When I was young, I would always go and watch the dance shows of my sister. As my sister was the oldest, she had the responsibility, of course, from a young age, to be the role model to her two younger brothers. So one day, I would go and watch somewhere far away. I sat in the car with my dad. You know, when you go on a Saturday in the car with your dad, just listening to the radio and being happy. You can stare out the window at the passing trees and being present with your dad. I just loved that when I was young and innocent. So, we were going to see my sister, Sissi, compete in this dancing competition. And that day, she won the competition and became Belgian champions with her dancing class. That day, she inspired me to become a champion. Little did I know that it would lead me to be Vice Olympic Champion, years later, at the Olympics in Rio.

I thanked her for being the role model she was, and still is. Then, the point where I got really emotional and barely could speak was when I started talking about the family company. My sister started working there for the family business. I said that I could really feel her presence in the company, and how it gave rest and peace for the family that the business is in good hands now. I thanked her for the way she did it, and I started crying again. Then she said that I may be the little brother, but that with my hockey career, I gave her a lot of energy also, to continue her life with her family (She's a mom of two children now.) and her job.

People don't really realise how much everyone is connected, and that doing your thing well impacts on everyone around you. It's scary sometimes but yet so powerful. I love the fact that by playing good and steaming on that right side of the field, it gives energy and inspiration to others. That is my greatest achievement so far, and why I love what I do. Looking for help and speaking it out is something that takes courage. Admitting that you need help, and accepting that other people have better ideas than you in some areas of life, is liberating. The ego is in the way, but you better kill it; at least if you want to lead a better and fulfilling life.

Mind

As I'm writing this book, choosing to walk this path and accepting the journey to write the book, a lot of interesting things happen. I stumble upon this podcast by Jim Kwik. I also follow one of his programs, Kwikreading, where he teaches you how to read *Kwikly*. I also listen to his podcast, Kwik Brain: the podcast about how to love your brain, Episode 54, blew me away. I'm sure it will blow you away too. I've written it down, sometimes with a small example of what it made me think about. The episode was made at the time of Valentine's Day. That's why he made one about *L.O.V.E. your brain*. And love your brain, you shall, because Jim Kwik believes, and therefore, I believe, that you can only love others as much as you love yourself. So start with your brain. And if you don't know where to start, go ask for help.

"Love your brain. The brain is the most powerful computer in the universe. I believe that you can only love a person to the degree that you love yourself. And a great place to start is loving your brain. Your brain is the control centre for all of your body and all of your functions, whether it's walking, talking, tasting, behaviour, reading, memory,..." says Jim Kwik. There are four keys to loving your brain. You need to nourish it so you flourish it. When you're struggling with your self-esteem or self-worth, loving your brain will make you show up as the best version of yourself and make you be unstoppable. And that's exactly what I want to be on the field.

Some facts: The brain roughly contains about a hundred billion brain cells. That's tremendous. You must know that there are 100 billion stars in the galaxy. Each of these neurons can transmit about a thousand nerve impulses per second, and can make as many as tens of thousands of synaptic connections with other neurons. A piece of your brain cell, as big as a grain of sand, contains like a hundred thousand neurons and one billion synapses, and they are all communicating with each other. And if you laid out the blood vessels that are feeding your brain, end to end, they would stretch out almost half way to the moon. Brain information travels about two hundred and sixty miles per hour, and is faster than most formula 1 race cars, which tap out at almost two hundred and forty miles per hour.

Your brain generates around 12 to 25 watts of electricity. Isn't that interesting? There's enough to power a low wattage LED light. The average brain is believed to have about 50 to 60 thousand thoughts per day. The only challenge is that 95 percent of those thoughts are the same thoughts you had yesterday or the day before that. The brain is capable of about a thousand or more processes per second, which makes it more powerful than any existing computer. You brain storage capacity is considered virtually unlimited. It doesn't get used up like ram in your computer.

How do you begin to L.O.V.E. your brain? The L stands for learn. The brain loves novelty, and loves new things to learn. So what are you learning? How often do you read? How often do you listen to podcasts? When do you go to classes? I started feeling really great when I started scheduling my reading time and podcast time. Usually, in Amsterdam, when I go to Albert Hein, I listen to a podcast while walking there. In the store, I have noticed that I couldn't figure out what I needed to buy because I couldn't focus on listening to the podcast and what I wanted to buy for food. I schedule my reading and writing in the morning; and especially when I just wake up, I like to read for a minimum of ten minutes. I do my morning meditation, and this makes my head clear of any negative thoughts about the day.

The second one is O, which stands for Oxygen. It's the food you eat, what you drink, the fresh air you take in, and the sunlight. The brain weighs around two percent of your bodyweight, but it uses about twenty percent of the resources: the energy, the oxygen, the nutrition. So, remember what you put in is what you get out. Take time to do your deep breathing. There's a lot you can do to feed the brain with more Oxygen, implementing the wider meaning of Oxygen. Is your diet in order? Are you watching the food that you put into your body? Especially for me, as an athlete, it's of the utmost importance to not have any injuries, to feed my brain, and to watch what I eat and drink. I need to make sure that I'm taking my supplements, and that I'm having fresh air.

Last week, I went sailing with my uncle on his boat. The funny thing was that I was yelling that I wanted a storm. I wanted to feel the wind, the waves, and the power of nature. I wanted to feel the higher power, and how small I actually am against the mighty forces of nature. It was between six and seven Beaufort. Nine Beaufort or more, on the scale of Beaufort, is a storm. It was intense, and we broke the beam shackle. I could feel my head being cleared by the wind. So I get what Jim Kwik is getting at: that your brain needs the good goodies. You get out what you put in.

One time, at Bloemendaal, we had a meeting on Tuesday about our game on Sunday. We played absolutely horrific. I couldn't stop any balls. There was no flow. There was just 18 men struggling along, not knowing what they were doing on the pitch. I scored a last minute goal, which was an amazing feeling, to get the win for the team. But during the meeting, we were discussing how we let it come so far. One of the arguments was that, on Friday, there was an event at Fanbased, a company Rogier Hoffman and Tim Jenniskens started, where they help people to deliver top performances based on knowledge from psychology, the military, and of course, top sport. The Friday evening, at the event in the Heineken House, we had a few drinks, and it was pretty late. So it was no surprise that on Sunday, there was a lot of hard work but no real effectiveness and quality.

I'm sometimes really frustrated when these things happen. But they happen. I said to the group that your body and mind is like a Ferrari formula 1 car. When you pour shit into it, it will not drive. Of course, half of the team laughed because it's typical of me to say those kinds of things, and it also sounds a bit childish. But I do it on purpose to make the message a bit lighter and not too serious. At the end of the year, when players leave the club, they need to give everyone a personalised present. This was half a year after I gave the Ferrari example. But they gave me a small Ferrari car—not a real one, sadly, but just a small, boy's plastic Ferrari. Using that example apparently was something they remembered. It didn't really have a great impact because most of them kept on drinking, which made me feel a bit sad.

The V stands for Vacation, meaning a digital break. So, no iPhone, email, or notifications whatsoever. New studies have shown that this is so important for your body and mind. Of course, a physical vacation is even better. But still, the digital break is a big one, because even when I was on vacation with my girlfriend, I still would put my phone on the table or take it with me to the beach, or use the maps to get me to a museum. In this way, your mind is constantly connected to a thousand possibilities, and tons of apps, and dozens of messages or snapchats or games, which makes the quality of your time with your partner or friend go dramatically down.

You can't be focused all the time. You need time to disconnect to be able to reconnect. Resting, relaxing, and disconnecting boosts your creativity and productivity, and decreases the chance of heart problems, stress, etc. Our devices are wiring us to be distracted and reactive, to be overloaded and overwhelmed, and to respond to everything that people need from us, with notifications and messages. So make sure you take time to unplug and relax. Also, sleep. There is an epidemic of sleeplessness. The brain needs rest to rejuvenate itself and clear out the stuff that leads to Alzheimer's and dementia.

Finally, the E stands for exercise. This is a bit of a no- brainer. As your body moves, your brain grooves. Exercise affects your brain on multiple fronts. It increases your heart rate. It pumps more oxygen to the brain. It also aids in the body's release of incredible amounts of positive hormones, all which participate in aiding and providing nourishing environments for the growth of new brain cells. Exercise stimulates the brain's plasticity. It stimulates growth, new connections, neurogenesis, and neuroplasticity, which accounts for a wide range of important neurotical activity areas of your brain. And there is a recent study done at UCLA that demonstrates that exercise increases the growth factors in your brain, making it easier for your brain to grow new neuro connections. It's kind of like our fertiliser—our Miracle-Gro, if you will—for your brain.

So, make sure you **L.O.V.E.** your brain: **Learn, Oxygen, Vacation**, take a little break from time to time, and **Exercise**. As your body moves, your brain grooves. And this is about love. As Jesus said, "Love yourself as you love your neighbour." Self-love and self-care is not selfish. It appreciates. It grows. It flourishes. So remember to love yourself. Follow your heart. And remember to take your brain with you.

Nothing is more common than unsuccessful people with talent.

Motivation

Les Brown is one of my big inspirations. I put his videos on YouTube, and they genuinely give me strength to move on, as I sometimes doubt if the path I'm taking is the right one because you can't see clearly in the future what will happen. I don't know what we will do at the World Cup. Well, it's important to know "why" you are doing it, whatever it is, because sometimes you are going to get tired. Sometimes you're going to get in a rut, where it seems like nothing goes right. For me, it's when I trained every single day, ate the right food, slept the right amount of hours, did my routines, and then, still, I didn't feel right and couldn't stop the ball, or my pass didn't seem to work. These were frustrating moments. But then, my "why" is so deeply engrained that whenever it gets tough, the tough get going. And that's me. Give me tough; give me weights; give me shuttles; give me tactics; give me critics—as much as you want—nothing is going to stop me. Nothing.

"The trouble with most of us is that we would rather be ruined by praise than saved by criticism." – Norman Vincent Peale

Writing

Writing this book was a step I took in January, after a breakdown with the national team. I had a problem. I would train Monday, Tuesday, Wednesday, Thursday, and Friday, and then have a game on Sunday. Raymond, my mentor for one year, asked me what I loved doing. It's actually a fun exercise. Let someone ask you what you love, and then you have to come up with an answer within 2 seconds. If you don't find an answer, the other person has to ask the question again. You can also repeat your answer. So let's say your answer is *food*. You can say *food* as many times as you want, if you can't find another answer. The thing is, you have to say what pops up in your mind immediately. Don't worry about what others think. Just say it. It can be funny.

I love going to the gym. I love exercising. I love being in the zone of creation. I love writing. I love reading. I love dancing. I love laughing. I love discussing. I love teams. I love food. I love oysters. I love my mom. I love my dad. I love my sister, my brother, my grandma, my team players. I love hitting the ball. I love loving. I love playing music. I love singing. I love, I love, I love. It doesn't mean I'm any good at it. Don't ever let someone tell you that you aren't any good at something. Someone's opinion of you doesn't have to become your reality. Then, see what you have been doing to all these things you love. Have you been giving your loves all the attention you should? Are there any passions you have that you have lost along the way?

For me, writing is the perfect relaxation between games and trainings, and during the preparation for the World Cup. Lately, I have been late for appointments. This week, I was 15 minutes late for the gym session and 10 minutes late for the team appointment. When I'm late, I'm not Emmanuel Stockbroekx, the Belgian International. I'm just the guy who comes late, which is horrible branding. I have built everything up, with good trainings, effort, and hard work. Being in the car for two hours, having stress of being late, and maybe getting a fine for speeding—all that has no point when you're late. Also, being on time is something I have to work on out of respect for my team and teammates, and out of self-respect.

PAY for the movies you watch and the music you listen to. Wouldn't you like to be paid for music you made? It feels good when you give to people who earned it. It makes you feel good.

Chapter 9

Learn Like a Maniac

Books

Frustrations of Teamwork

Lencioni wrote a book about the five frustrations of teamwork. I have been playing on teams all my life. I am now playing on the national team and Bloemendaal, and consider myself to be a professional because I'm paid for doing sports. That's the official explanation. But also, I think it's necessary that people work together, and that they cross the line between them and the others. Working together can be powerful. It can move mountains and give inspiration and energy to others.

Sports can be bigger than life itself when some principles are met, guidelines are followed, and people trust each other and are committed. It has come to my attention that the frustrations Patrick Lencioni talks about are the exact frustrations I have as well, with the teams I play on. Of course, these are frustrations about teamwork. There are a lot of things I'm grateful for while being part of the teams I'm on. As I made a choice to be accountable for the success of the teams I play on, I have become aware of these frustrations and, sadly, they are everywhere around us. But you can play a very big role in making those frustrations turn into opportunities, and to have breakthroughs and grow as a person. As Gandhi said, *"You must be the change you wish to see in the world."* It is easier said than done; it's hard.

Going for a vision you have means people won't necessarily like you, at least not in the beginning. It will mean being alone and being frustrated because people don't understand you and the feelings you have. But often, the fear of doing the hard stuff is just an illusion. As Les Brown famously quoted, *"Do what is easy, and your life will be hard. Do what is hard, and your life will be easy."* I always think about the movie, *Shawshank Redemption,* where Andy Dufresne (Tim Robbins) has to go through hell, literally, and through five hundred yards of pure shit before he reaches freedom. I think, sometimes in life, you also have to go through a big pile of shit, whether you like it or not. Sadly, sometimes it's the only way to your freedom. But when you find teammates and can find ways to work together and commit to a cause greater than yourself, life becomes easy. Still, you'll have hard moments, but those moments you must learn from.

Lack of Trust

There is nothing cheesier than stating that trust is important in a team. But what does it mean? It's a bit the same as saying breakfast is the foundation of having a great day. Or, as Benjamin Franklin quotes, *"Early to bed and early to rise, makes a man healthy, wealthy, and wise."* Still, how many people do you know that don't do it, who know it's important and still don't do it? You know that having a cell phone beside your bed is bad for your sleep, but you still leave the phone hanging around. You know that even one glass of alcohol is bad for you, shown by recent studies, but you still drink wine. There is something about us humans; it's interesting. What is it that ignites the will to do something?

I can understand when people have a normal job and do these things on social occasions, but not when you're preparing for something such as a World Cup or the Olympics, and you still have trouble not drinking, not smoking, and going to bed early and getting up early. I think that shows mental weakness, not being able to have the discipline to do the right things—the small things—because the small things become the big things. I noticed that it was exactly those moments where I disciplined myself and my thinking, and they were moments where I grew. I was aware of my decisions having an influence on my life, and now it's an addiction. The process of getting better is really addictive. When you do those small things right, you build trust in yourself. People around you will trust you, and you will feel it. It's the first step to being successful, or creating a successful team. It starts with you.

"Whoever is careless with the truth in small matter cannot be trusted with important matters." – Albert Einstein

Fear of Conflicts

You probably had some discussions about lifestyle in your life. Some players find it important to live an ascetic lifestyle. Some players eat two snickers before training. Some players skip their breakfast. Some players eat cereal. Some players see the energy you can get from food, and they make power smoothies and power meals. Some can't eat the healthy vegetables you need to eat. You might see food as something that needs to please you, and you need to have that good feeling when you eat, where the flavors stick in your mouth. Or that feeling you get after dinner, let's say between 9 and 12 at night, where you're watching your favorite show or movie, and you just need those sweets or M&M's, or those nacho chips or ice cream. And you realise, after twenty minutes, the whole bag is empty. You have that voice that's telling you to eat some more and that it's good for you, and that you deserved it.

Priests live an ascetic lifestyle. An ascetic person has a way of life that is simple and strict, usually because of their religious beliefs. They are also characterized by abstinence of sensual pleasures, often for the purpose of pursuing spiritual goals. I've seen players with the biggest talent, drinking beers and putting their health and physique on the line. I wonder what the psychology behind this is. I understand that some believe that it can create a strong bond between players. It's important to talk about those things with your team. Usually, after an intense moment like a game or a fight, things come up. For example, when there are frustrations during or after a training, because a guy you don't like on your team said something to you at training. He had some criticism about the way you were going about your business or training. And you just couldn't bear one word coming out of his mouth.

It's important to talk about those things in a healthy way. As in a family, where brothers and sisters fight as well, you need to stop the cycle. When you're having bitterness towards someone or something because they did you wrong, write it down. Then watch if there is something you or he/she can do about it; or talk about it with someone—someone with some expertise in that matter. Ask him how he saw the situation. Be interested in what he was feeling and interpreting so you can go into his world and understand why he reacted in the way he did. If not, let it go. Don't let it affect you any longer. Don't let someone control your life.

I believe that in order to achieve a better you, why not give it all you've got. I've made it a habit to give more of myself than what I'm paid to do. A lot of people just do what is necessary in order to not get fired. Become the best version of yourself, and don't leave any chance or room for distractions. Become single-minded to achieve the goals you want to achieve. Do what is necessary, day in and day out, in order to achieve what you want. It's important to know your goal. What is your goal? Where do you see yourself in one year? In two years? In five years? Or ten years? Becoming stronger, faster, and smarter? More loveable? Having more skills in a certain area? Becoming more competitive in the marketplace? For your goal or your dream, have a plan and stick to it. Eat healthy. Sleep on time. And when you do these things, when you learn to say no, the thing that you are actually learning is self-discipline and self-mastery.

You need the same self-discipline and focus during training, during exercises, and during life. And when you reach that point of self-discipline, you feel in control. You are the master of your body, and not the other way around. What I found difficult is when players have a different view on this and don't see the benefit of self-discipline outside the pitch. When they don't meet the same standards as I do, I could become very frustrated about this. But then again, I also needed to learn that some players have different goals and dreams than I have. Yet again, I learned that by talking and listening to every player on my team, and getting to know them better. I also learned that a lot of people have the same desires.

A recent research, conducted by Motivation Factor and analysed by Boston Research Group, came up with some interesting insights in the differences between what drives men and women. You want to be great at something—a great father, great entrepreneur, an adventurer; an inventor; a great mother and grandmother; a great artist or athlete; a great dancer or singer; a great friend, brother, or sister; a great speaker—there are lots of things where you can achieve greatness, for men or for women. But there are some differences between what is important and how you achieve that greatness within you.

For men, it's important to succeed, to achieve the goals they set out to achieve, to know the truth, to take the initiative or take the lead, and to be brave.

While for women, it's more important to find balance, to use intuition, and to listen to others. They have the need to feel respected, and they have empathy towards each other.

For example, I could easily say, "We are preparing for the World Cup. In order to achieve an athletic body to my greatest potential, I will not drink or smoke." And then, someone will say, "Not even one beer after the game, or on Sunday (which would become three, four, or more beers)?" I would say, "No. Not even when I have dinner with my family, and everybody is drinking wine; or at a party at my friend's, where everybody is having a good time, enjoying the worry-free student life." Then I would say again, "No, not even then, and especially not then, because then, I am tested." I would have to say no to someone proposing a beer, at least ten times.

Your dream and your goal is tested. If you say yes, even just once, it might be that you pushed your dream away for another year, or for even more years, without you even realising it. They start saying, "Yeah, but everybody is different." Or, "Let everybody decide for themselves." And sure, I get that. Everybody is different. But don't we all have the same goals? Aren't we all on the same team, striving towards a goal? Let's say, for example, to have a happy, healthy life? In my life, it's simple. It's literally a goal, and usually a big tournament, like the Olympics or the World Cup, or the game on Sunday. It gives my life a great deal of structure and perspective and purpose. And I can tell you, when we were at the Olympics, you could just feel that everybody was going for that same goal. Everybody on that team made the sacrifices. They stopped their job or studies to focus fully on the Olympic team. Everybody had a strong will and the belief that we could achieve something at the Olympics. And when you do have that in your team, where everybody goes through fire for each other, that's where you feel alive! You feel you can move mountains; you tap into your greatness, and you start flowing.

As Maslow suggests in his diagram, there are seven levels a person should go through during his life—call it transition, or call it growth: physiological, safety, belongingness and love, esteem, self-actualization, and self-transcendence.

I think there are some basics that you need to mindful of, which are there for everyone. Having a conflict often leads to new insights and better, deeper relationships, which you need on the pitch and in life. Because you go very deep together, you have to be willing to run for the other. And when some things are left unspoken, or some things are still lying in your stomach, they fester and grow into ugly, nasty spots, like pimples you don't treat well. They lead to frustration, bitterness, and worst of all, regret. Listen to your heart. Let it speak. Don't let people who are addicted to mediocrity decide what is best for you.

It's not easy. As in sports, it's usually about philosophy and how you feel towards the game: what are you willing and not willing to leave out? What sacrifices are you willing to make? Are you willing to go the extra mile, or not? Are you willing to fight for the extra 10 %? With everything, it's in the last ten percent that you find the greatest joy—the mile that not many people want to walk, and the path many people avoid: rocks, thorns, pain…

Lack of Commitment

You get out what you put in. How hard can you let that sink in? What YOU get out is what YOU put in. So, when you put love in your craft, people will love your craft. When you hate your craft, people will hate your craft. When you are stressful with your craft, people will have stress seeing you or your craft. When you are not putting effort into what you want, people won't put any effort toward helping you. Or they'll just say that it just isn't hitting it. You don't get that warm fuzzy feeling. Your commitment starts with you and with no one else. Have commitment to take action. Have commitment to act on your ideas. Have commitment to have courage.

The greats, like Van Gogh, Mozart, Einstein, Steve Jobs, Abraham Lincoln, Maradona, Michael Jordan, Messi…they aren't just their names. They are Apple, they are music, they are art, they are football… they are it. They were fully embedded in what they did. They literally were what they did. They transcended normal life. They made life seem that much brighter and better, and they gave inspiration.

Let's say Fred (who is a fictive person) is feeling pretty negative today. He hasn't slept well. He had a fight with his wife about not spending enough time with her because he is frustrated how things are going at his work. He doesn't get fulfilment from what he is doing. He has great visions of what it could be; but somehow, his team isn't inspiring whatsoever, and they don't have the same energy and standards they should have. So then, Fred goes to work with a heavy bag on his back already. But Fred goes, fired up to work, because he realises that maybe this job can save him from his life where he feels miserable most of the time. He has great hopes that this day will give him what he desires to achieve his dreams. But then he needs to do an exercise or workshop, or training or meeting, and he finds the meeting stupid and unproductive. He doesn't feel that he gets better from the training.

Because Fred wants to get better, he goes searching outside his world, where he'll find the magic sprinkles that will make him be the person he wants to be. He waits and looks and hunts, like a lion hunts his prey, silently crawling, steadily moving forward, with the biggest focus. He is single-mindedly going towards his prey, his goal, not getting distracted. Then, in an instant, he goes into a full sprint, jumping, and using his claws to take down his prey. He is being relentless, taking a life for his, and he is fully committed.

A lot of people think that they'll find the magic outside, and that's partly true. You'll have to get out of bed and go to work, or go to training, to school, or classes. Or to the supermarket to buy food to survive. But the biggest mistake you can make is that you then wait until things just happen, wandering around and hoping for the best. At one point, you'll have to realise that you get out what you put in; that you have to be committed yourself, to grow, learn, and get better, and to have the mindset that the magic you search for is inside you. You have to realise that you have to make the exercise work; that you have to make the day work for you instead of you working for the day; that things don't happen to you but for you; that the challenges you face now, you'll have always; that sometimes you're up and sometimes you're down, and that's just part of life; and that sometimes life will feel like a hard, cold, nasty thing: an uppercut; a raise you don't get; a promotion you worked for, for years, but someone with far less experience gets it. But that feeling or mood is just something that's in you. Don't let it control everything. It's important to know that you will project that feeling outwards to the world.

So, when I feel bad, and I go to training with that bad feeling, I will be tempted to say that the training was bad, or that I didn't get out of it what I wanted, or that some players irritated me. And that is something I need to be mindful of.

Be committed to make it work—to make it happen; to make what you are doing work—and not the other way around. Don't think the work you'll do will make you. Life won't change until you change.

Avoidance of Accountability

"The best kind of accountability on a team is peer-to-peer. Peer pressure is more efficient and effective than going to the leader, anonymously complaining, and having them to stop what they are doing to intervene." – Patrick Lencioni

Ludo is on a team, and Ludo finds it important that the team is one. Everybody is on the same page, striving towards the same goal. He sees it reflecting in every part of his life. He sleeps for his team. He dreams about the team. He realises that his team is a role model for others. He's not afraid to take the lead in certain matters—he does everything for the team. Then, one day, Ludo sees that a certain part of the group has a different WhatsApp group, besides the team's WhatsApp, where everybody is in.

Certain team members live in a certain area together, and they often meet and drink coffee together. Ludo, who also would like to be part of that social group and live those moments together, feels hurt. He doesn't feel part of the group anymore, and he feels that some guys hang out with others more. He also thinks this is not good for the atmosphere of the group. At one point, Alfred, who is in that coffee WhatsApp group, and part of that strong group within the group, talks to Ludo. You have to know that Ludo is afraid to speak up about these feelings. He is scared that talking about those feelings, and showing his vulnerability, would mean he would get hurt, because guys within that strong group would call what he was saying, *ridiculous*. They would say that thinking like that is stupid, and that the group grew naturally, and that it's just how it is. Basically, they would just ignore how Ludo feels. What they forget is that Ludo has a bigger purpose. He wants everybody to be in the circle and to feel included in the team.

For example, during tournament, the coffee group would go out for a coffee during free time. And then they would post on Instagram how much fun they were having, which is completely normal. But Ludo would feel lonely. He would feel not wanted. Some other team players didn't think much of it; they were just happy that they were having a good time and could enjoy themselves. But Ludo wants to be part of it. He feels like an outsider at those moments. Ludo talks to other team members, and he hears that they also feel that it's not good for the team, and that everybody should be invited for coffee. They also feel like outsiders sometimes.

Ludo decides, in agreement with the team coach, that this matter should be talked about within the group. He arranges a time when the whole team is present, and he starts talking about how he feels and why he feels that way. As you can expect, there is George, who reacts like it isn't a problem, and he rolls his eyes, followed by a big sigh. David doesn't even look at Ludo when he speaks, because David finds that those things come naturally, and he doesn't have any problem with anything. He doesn't want to control anything or anyone. Hugo is very happy that Ludo talks, because he feels the same way. But because Hugo is one of the younger team members, nobody really listens to him, although he has a very good view on things.

Patrick, who is really concerned about how everyone feels, is really encouraging Ludo to speak up. Patrick wants to play for a successful team, and knows that it is important that everybody's feelings are respected and taken seriously into consideration. He knows that this empowers people and that good will come out of it, even if it means that you have to go into conflict for a time (of course, in a healthy way). What Patrick is frustrated with (He was in the coffee WhatsApp group but deliberately removed himself from the group because he heard that some players weren't happy with it.) is that some of the driving forces in the group don't take the accountability to change some of the behaviours. They are afraid of change. They take it personally and don't see the bigger picture of having the opportunity to make everyone feel part of the group and to eventually grow as a team. The payoffs for their present behaviour are greater than the payoffs of a changed behaviour. But Ludo put it out on the table. He had the courage to speak up. And therefore, the first step is taken towards a better team. And that is what leaders do. They speak up.

Inattention to Results

You have human rights—rights inherent to all human beings— regardless of sex, race, nationality, ethnicity, language, religion, or any other status. Human rights include the right to life and liberty, freedom from slavery and torture, freedom of opinion and expression, the right to work and education, and many more. As you and I have these rights, there comes a time of duty. Knowledge is not power; it is potential power. Only if you use your attained knowledge, then you shall have power over your life. Too many of us do not use the information and the knowledge at hand.

It is like when you read the menu in the restaurant and you look at the steak with salad and French fries. You look at it, you read it, you understand it, and you probably have an image in your mind of the steak. You picture yourself eating the steak. You may start thinking about where it comes from. You start thinking about friends you know who are vegan. You start thinking that maybe you should not order this steak. Or you don't think about those types of things, and you search further. There is a difference between reading the menu and actually eating and experiencing the food. You ordering your food is your right, because you are going to pay for it. You earned your money, hopefully, in the right way. But the cook has a duty to fulfil, which is to make that dish for you. The waiter's duty is to get the orders for the guests and serve the food, and behave in such a way that the guests feel at ease during their stay in the restaurant, and they go home feeling satisfied.

As a player, no matter what sport, you play with your name on your back. Your name is attached to the result you will attain. Whether you end up fifth, sixth, or first, your name is attached to it. You have these players who end up doing something and not caring about the results. Or they'll say it's the referees' fault that they lost, or that you don't have the right players on your team, or the right circumstances. They stay at the same level. They're not stretching, not growing, and they become very cynical and negative about life. They throw in the towel, on themselves and on their dreams. They don't care about the results anymore, and they end up stuck, not knowing they are the captain of their soul—the master of their fate.

Being the Ideal Team Player

For an athlete, being humble, driven, and smart is as equally important as speed, power, and coordination. They make all the rest easy. When you do the extra mile, life becomes easy. When you reach a certain level, and when you reach a certain depth in what you do, there is not a lot of competition left. There is a place where not many dare to go, because it will make you stand out. It might embarrass you, and it will make your face make funny expressions, like in the gym when you're lifting heavy weights. And you start sweating and making funny noises. That's where some will stop because they care more about what others think of them than to go for what they want.

If we would all strive to be the ideal team player, wouldn't that be wonderful? Being humble is a nice one, I believe. It is something that is needed, especially when you have that first success; it is necessary to stay humble. You never know how much the other person also worked for it but had some bad luck. Be humble in victory and gracious in defeat. Be smart. Think. Think about what you do. Be obsessed with how to get better, and see opportunities where you can grow. I'm writing this book to grow myself: to finish a project, to keep my mind focused and disciplined, to learn new things, to experiment, to be driven, and to be the best I possibly can be every day. Maybe there will be days where it seems impossible, but get through them anyhow. Get it done. Get the job done, whatever it takes. Never give up. When 99% are saying it can't be done, be the one percent that says it can be done.

Jesus

It is funny because, for my whole life, I have been saying my prayer with Jesus in it, the one I made with my dad. But what does Jesus stand for? I read a book that I found at the Boekenbeurs, in Antwerp: *Jesus, the Mysticus from Adyashanti*. There are people in the world who find salvation in Jesus Christ. They say they can get through anything with Jesus Christ on their side, as though He can be their companion on the lonely road some of them have, or a part of their life when they can't find any purpose or direction. Jesus spread the gospel of faith, love, and forgiveness. You'll say, "Yeah, that's easy. Sure, love is nice."

Faith, I understand. When you play a game, you also have some faith that you'll win it. Some will go very far to prove that point. And forgiveness is easy. I've forgiven many times. One time, I had an accident with my car because someone crossed the road while the light was red. I had to pay 800 euros for a new bumper. Even though I had insurance, I still had to pay 800 euros. I jumped out of the car and yelled to the man crossing the street, who had caused the car in front of me to shut his brakes down, and for me to drive into the back of his car. "You stay here, man!" The moment he saw my anger, he started to run away. It was in the middle of the street and next to the bus stop, so everyone was watching.

It must have been a sight: first, seeing an accident; then, seeing the driver get out of his car and yell at the pedestrian who had crossed the street while the light was red; and then, the pedestrian sprinting away. I realised that I let my anger get the best of me. I was furious; I can remember. Now, I forgive him. It's something that happened. I believe that you have to take personal responsibility when something happens to you. I realise I was too close to the car in front of me and wasn't really paying attention. But did I really, really forgive the guy? Forgive but not forget, maybe.

People end up hating or resenting someone for the rest of their life. Not realising that a certain person is causing your frustration and anger, when you are not able to forgive, it's like you are drinking a glass of poison every day. Choose love and forgiveness. In meditation, it is about focusing on your inner flame and your breath, and being aware of yourself. When you have this awareness, you can easily go to the person, thing, or event for which you have frustrations or anger towards. Imagine that there is a string or a rope connecting you to that person or event. Now, imagine taking scissors and cutting it right through. You just let it go. You no longer let it affect you, because now you realise, even though you have every right to be angry, that person really did you wrong. The one suffering the most is you. It's like pouring a glass of poison, every day, into your soul.

Once, I was on a train, on my way to World Youth day. I went with my brother and father. It was in 2005, in Germany, Cologne. It was the first foreign trip of Pope Benedict XVI. The World Youth day, in 2016,

Krakow, Poland, was attended by three million people, and was led by Pope Francis. I was on the train. It was like going on a pilgrimage. You need to take the train, and then walk several hours. In Cologne, there were one million people. At night, Pope Benedict XVI gave his service. I remember that I was on something higher. I could see a big part of the one million people. The sun had gone down, and the service was given on some type of hill, and it was lit up. There, stood the pope and all the cardinals, on a lighted hill. Everyone was sitting on the ground. And then the pope asked everyone to light their candles. You could see this sea of people lighting up their candles. I remember this so well. It was one of the most beautiful things I had ever seen. I was realising that to light up your flame, you must first light it up. You have to give it the spark. And then it will grow and grow.

Superconscious

I looked it up, and here is an answer regarding Nayaswami Parvati. Nayaswami Parvati is one of Ananda's most widely travelled and experienced ministers. With her husband, Nayaswami Pranaba, she helped to create and direct Ananda centers in Palo Alto, Portland, Seattle, Dallas, and Assisi, Italy. Ananda is dedicated to the belief that you can live in joy. They teach effective techniques for expanding your sense of self, such as meditation, Kriya yoga, spiritual Hatha yoga, and divine friendship. The *conscious* mind is what we operate with during our daily activities and waking hours. It represents only a small portion of our consciousness and awareness.

The *subconscious* mind lies below the level of conscious awareness. Its physical seat in the body is the lower brain and the spine. It records everything we do: every activity we engage in, our thoughts about those activities, and our likes and dislikes about what we encounter each day. Although nothing is forgotten by the subconscious mind, for the most part, this part of our consciousness remains hidden from our everyday awareness. The subconscious has a tremendous influence on how we think and act when in the conscious state.

The *superconscious* mind encompasses a level of awareness that sees both material reality and also the energy and consciousness behind that reality.

If we have a really good meditation and feel *fully calm* as you have stated, then we are beginning to experience a level of *super-consciousness*. As we go deeper in meditation and experience a deepening peace, calmness, divine love, and even bliss, then we are experiencing deeper levels of the superconscious. The superconscious is where true creativity is found. Expressions of this kind of creativity are distinctive from those that come from the subconscious. The superconscious is where ideas for truly great works of art, music, prose, poetry, great scientific discoveries, and deep spiritual experiences are found. Paramhansa Yogananda made an interesting statement. He said that *"thoughts are universally, not individually, rooted."* This means that as we elevate our consciousness and access the superconscious, we are accessing the thoughts that live on that level of consciousness. These thoughts don't belong to us but are *universally* available to those who live more on that level of consciousness.

The opposite is also true. If we live mainly on the conscious or subconscious level, then we attract the kinds of thoughts that live on those levels of consciousness.

Generally speaking, the conscious mind sees everything as separate from each other. A chair is only a chair; a person is simply the body they inhabit and nothing more. It has a very limited view of the world around it.

The superconscious mind sees that everything is, in reality, made of energy and consciousness and, therefore, it sees the underlying unity behind the outer forms.

The subconscious mind consists of *"the unprocessed residue of thoughts, actions, and memories that are ever present, but more or less unnoticed. They greatly influence the conscious mind, which doesn't often realize how ungoverned by free will its decisions really are.*" (*Awaken to Superconsciousness,* by Swami Kriyanda) In other words, the subconscious influences a lot of what we do each day, but those influences are from past actions and the habits we have created from them. This means that ideas that are drawn from the subconscious are not going to be new and creative. Looking in the subconscious can be like rummaging around in the closet to see what we've stored away. This is why the usual dream state often has a confused and murky feel to it. There are also superconscious dreams, but they will have an uplifting and life-changing effect on us, and feel quite different from the usual dreams we may have.

Letting It Go

When I am coming towards a tournament, I get really tense. Everything has to be perfect. I want to be in control. It's good to be in control of my own stuff. But when I then look around and see things that I would not do, I project my belief onto others or other things, so my norm would become the norm of others. This is where the yoga and meditation helped me. I get it when psychologists say, "Let it go," or, "You are not the norm." I truly get that, but I would still have that nagging feeling. With meditating, it's gone. I truly feel I let it go, and I feel myself in this super-state, feeling creative, powerful, and ready to take new action.

When your BODY moves
Your BRAIN grooves.

BUY a TRAMPOLINE
Jump on it in the morning. Ten minutes can have a huge
impact on your day.
It helps your lymphatic system to do its job.
The lymph system, which carries toxic substances out of
your body, needs gravity and body movement to work
properly. Bouncing on a trampoline stimulates the
lymphatic drainage system to get rid of toxins, bacteria, and
waste from your cells, effectively cleansing them.
It improves energy levels.
More oxygen flows around your body when you bounce on a
trampoline, and this can result in a rise in energy levels.
Meanwhile, getting extra oxygen to your brain can improve
mental alertness.
Having a trampoline in your house is also just nice to have.
When things get too serious, just jump on it and see what
happens.

It's good for relieving stress and boosting your mood.
Exercise, such as trampolining, will release endorphins, the
feel-good brain chemicals.
These can help to reduce stress and ease anxiety and
depression. It's fun and can leave you feeling invigorated.
So, can you give me a reason why not to do it??
Thought so.

And while you are at it, BUY A SPINNER.
Do extra sessions, four times, for eight minutes, with your
heart rate at 60 % of your maximum heart rate. Do it while
listening to motivational videos or motivational music.

Chapter 10

Miracles

Life

"The thoughtless, the ignorant, and indolent, seeing only the apparent effects of things and not the things themselves, talk of law, of fortune, and chance. Seeing a man grow rich, they say, 'How lucky he is!' Observing another become intellectual, they exclaim, 'How highly favored he is!' And noting the saintly character and wide influence of another, they remark, 'How chance aids him at every turn!' They don't see the trials and failures and the struggles that these men have voluntarily encountered in order to gain their experience; have no knowledge of the sacrifices they have made, of the undaunted efforts they have put forth, of the faith they have exercised, that they might overcome the apparently insurmountable, and realize the vision of their heart. They do not know the darkness and the heart aches; they only see the light and the joy, and they call it 'luck;' do not see the longing arduous journey, but only behold the pleasant goal, and call it 'good fortune;' do not understand the process, but only perceive the result, and call it 'chance.'"

You know those people who see a great player make a last minute goal, and they call it *luck*. Or they see celebrities in a movie and say, "If only I could have the opportunity to play in a movie." They say words like *chance*, *luck*, and *good fortune*. It was when I had given a presentation

149

at a joint venture event of two companies, Cipal and Schaubroeck, the IT partners for governments. Besides data centre services, they also do managed services, IT-consultancy, and audits.

Basically, my 25-minute presentation or story was about how two cultures can come together and work together as we did with the Red Lions at the Olympics, being one of, if not the best Olympic hockey team of the Rio Olympics. We were relentless in every area and became Vice Olympic champion, something no other Belgian team had ever done before in the history of the Olympics. People were shocked by the level of our play. Knowing that two cultures, the French and the Flemish, were working fiercely for each other in the heat of the battle, Cipal and Schaubroeck wanted to know the secrets of our success. Cipal and Schaubroeck were once competitors and now realised that working together would bring greater opportunities, not only for themselves but also for others.

So I did my talk for about 25 minutes. Afterwards, at the reception, a woman came to me and said: "If only my son could be more like you." I was stunned because it was a stranger giving me an indirect compliment. A compliment in my mind was very weird because, in my mind, I was still the guy who stopped going to school, didn't go to college, and still lives at his parents' house. But I must say that when I was on stage and was flowing my energy in the room about my passion for the game and my team, I never felt so good in my life. Then, suddenly, I thought, "Well, maybe you should help her son in whatever way." And I realised I was having a conversation with myself. I said, "Well, I have no clue; how? And who am I to help that mother, whose son has no real motivation or passion for anything? I'm just a simple guy playing hockey. I have no degree or master."

I also got lots of cards from people who wanted me to come and talk at their organisation or sports club. I had no idea that my talk could have such a big impact on people. And never would I have thought that people would give their cards and/or credentials. A man came to me and started talking about his music band he was in, and that he had felt the same way I felt, that when you are playing and get into a certain flow state, you are experiencing something greater than yourself. It was a very special moment. I realised that what I was doing was somehow meaningful to a lot of people, although I still felt inferior to all those people. The two CEOs were sitting in the front row, and I was speaking to them. I had to keep my feet on the ground because it was something I didn't really expect ever to happen in my life.

Change is something people fear. What if the behaviour and habits and beliefs you have, unconsciously, would have to change—the stuff you do on a day-to-day basis? The life you've built up is a life that doesn't add up to anything. You are just consuming but not creating. You are doing your job, having the same thoughts about work every day—I have to look after this mail, and this call; again, an angry customer, and that client that didn't pay; those open accounts; that lawsuit; my competition is stealing clients; the IT company is working slow; that colleague is making too many mistakes—and every day, it's the same song, and nothing much changes. Eventually, you get numb and hope someone else is going to fix it. The decisions you make are bad decisions. You constantly say that you are unlucky, or that you just don't have the right resources or the right circumstances to be successful. *"Men do not attract what they want but what they are."* That is a quote from the book, *As a Man Thinketh*, by James Allen. I like this quote. You can read it and say, "This is just another stupid quote, such as, *"As you sow, so shall you reap,"* from the Bible, Galatians VI (King James Version). But few people really see what it means. In a deeper sense of the quote, it means you take full responsibility for your life, and for your dreams, your circumstances, your feelings, and your thoughts.

As I was eating with some friends yesterday, as a guest, we were eating these wonderful home cooked mussels with handmade French fries. There is something special about handmade food. You feel and taste the love the host put into it for his guests. He took the time to make a wonderful dish. You can feel that he is proud that he made those tasty French fries, unlike when I get the French fries from the same old take-out where I have gone my whole life, where they still don't say "hi," or even know my name. They are the most unpassionate, dull people. But still, you end up going there for some reason. Maybe it is because they keep it simple, without too much fuss, which you eventually start appreciating. Or maybe I'm trying to justify their behaviour, which, maybe, is just unacceptable.

Anyway! In the beginning of the evening, it was a bit awkward because the son of the host was home after being away a long time from home for study and work. He got fired and didn't do much more than consume the money of his father, having a good time—a typical example of young men not having a purpose and not really knowing what to do. They are just consuming. The father, like any father, would help his son by giving a certain amount of money. And there is nothing wrong with that. But the only thing the father would ask in return was that his son call him three times every month. As it turned out, he called him once every three months, checking if his father would still be willing to pay his bills, and putting up every lie he could so he could just continue his life.

To be fair, it's hard in this life. When you are not feeling well or are in the grip of a bad experience, you tend to get stuck in a way. You get cynical and negative about life. The more problems you have, the more you seem to attract them. And without you even knowing it, you are digging your own hole. Also, the parents of the host were there after a long time of not seeing them. And there were some others as well. When the starters, some olives and tapenades with dips, were on the table, I took the time to go around with the little plate of starters. It creates a smile when you give people something just for the sake of giving, and it is something that gives me a great sense joy, doing it just for the sake of doing it. That feeling is more valuable than all the gold in the world. It brings a light in the room. Then, when we were finishing our dinner, there was dessert: ice cream from the famous

Cocorico, the best ice cream of Brasschaat. People stand in line for hours just to have a scoop of Cocorico. You can also buy white, 1-litre buckets of ice. And so they were presented on the table.

I stood up and announced that I would give everybody a bowl of ice. This was something that just came to me, a little voice saying that I should do it because nobody was really moving. Still, I was a guest and did not have to do it. As I was scooping away, I felt a kind of joy and happiness come inside me, and this I could see with the other family members. They were all smiling and making jokes as I was scooping, enjoying the fact that I was asking them what they wanted, and making the scoops with great love and diligence.

The man of the house complimented me at least three times, and said how much he appreciated the fact I was giving the ice to everyone. Meanwhile, I was thinking, "This is just normal, no? Nothing special." But then, it hit me. It is special. It is something small. As it goes, "When you can't do great things, do small things in a great way." And so I realised, by being of service to the people around you, taking the initiative with the right motives, it can have a big impact on the people around you and yourself. And even if it's just a small scoop of ice, it can bring joy and happiness. *"As a man thinketh, so is he." "As you sow, so shall you reap."*

Inspirations

Today, a boy came to me. He goes to school where we are preparing for the World Cup in Brussels. When we were training out on the field, our locker room was open, and my audio box was standing there. It is an orange Bose box. I left it there during our training, already having the feeling on the pitch that I shouldn't have left it there.

When we returned from the field, the box was gone. And immediately, we knew that it was one of the boys from the school who took it, because they passed by our locker rooms on Mondays. They must have taken it. I went to the club manager and told him that it was stolen, and I asked if they could just ask the students to give it back. I wasn't feeling any resentment, and I wasn't angry. I was feeling rather sorry for the boy who had taken it because I knew he had just made a bad decision. They said they would go and try to figure out who took the box.

Now, this was two weeks ago. And today, the boy came to me. He gave it back and said he was sorry. He looked at the ground and was feeling rather embarrassed, I think. Then I laid my hand on his shoulder. By this act, he looked at me and smiled. And there I saw, in his eyes, that he had good in him. I smiled and said I was happy that he made the good decision to give it back.

These little inspirations in life are things that give me energy. This young boy will grow into a man one day, and the world will need him in a good way. In this way, he will have learned a lesson that you can be forgiven and start again. It is important that we have a forgiving heart to those who make mistakes. As for the boy, maybe he was pressured by his peers to steal. Maybe he was never able to have a sound box. Sometimes we are caught by a bad spirit and bad thoughts. But we can always find a moment to get back on the right track. This boy was an inspiration to me.

Habits

"Good habits made at youth make all the difference." – Aristotle

A habit is something you do often or regularly, without you even knowing it. It can be a habit like always buying the same toothpaste, or the habit of putting sugar in your coffee. It can be shaking someone's hand when you see them, or smiling or frowning when you are thinking. It can be picking your nose in the car, where no one will see you picking your nose because you're in the car (while actually, everyone can see you very clear). Or it can be the physical pain you feel when you need another hit of cocaine, not that I have ever done this. But you often see TV programs about people who are addicted. They literally go into prostitution to be able to buy another shot of drugs so that they will not feel the pain. It can be different things.

The thing about a habit is that you notice yourself doing it unconsciously. When you are conscious of your habit, you are aware of the impact it has on others around you and on yourself. As in Matthew, Chapter 7, Verse 12, *"So in everything, do to others what you would have them to do to you, for this sums up the Law and the Prophets."*

So, when you look at your day, what are your habits? Which of them are helping you towards your goal? For example, I must drink at least two liters of water a day because, one, I'm big, 1m90, and I lose a lot of water during my training. And mostly, I train two times a day. When you don't drink enough water, your performance level can drop down to twenty percent. That is huge, especially when I go to India with the national team, where it will be hotter than usual; although Bhubaneswar is not that hot, I have to drink a lot of water.

What most of us don't know is that it isn't necessarily your muscles that need water; they do need water, but your brain needs lots of hydration too. It uses more energy than any other human organ. The energy is used for the electrical impulses between neurons. While you do sports, the brain uses a lot of this energy, because you're focused on many things; you need to move, and your body is sweating. You use every inch of your body, and you need your brain to react to the circumstances on the pitch.

The brain uses up to twenty percent of your total energy haul. When the brain doesn't have enough hydration, it will get dehydrated. Think of a piece of steak that has been overcooked. It's just useless. So then your brain will send you a message to stop whatever you're doing. That's why most people, when they begin to work out, have to stop.

It's not because the body is tired, or the basic condition is low, which can definitely be the case with some. But even I, when I'm not well hydrated, can't perform at the level I'm used to performing at. It is also important to not overhydrate yourself.

Ideas

"Great minds discuss ideas. Average minds discuss events. Small minds discuss people." – Eleanor Roosevelt. Ideas do change the world. But whether it is a good one, that is the question. There have been people who forced their ideas into this world, onto people, with a lot of consequences. But some ideas were brilliant, like the umbrella. You have people who complain about the rain. You have people who just get wet and get on with it. And then you have people who invent the umbrella.

There were people who invented sailing, combining human intelligence and nature into an art form. My father likes to sail. Often, we would go on a sailing trip with the family. That has been for a long time. My father always compares life with sailing boats. It's funny. I think it was last week when he advised me on how you form a healthy relationship just as you would create a good boat. You need a big sail, and a good draft. If the draft is not well put and balanced, the ship has no use. What is your course? How is the wind blowing? Is it in your favour? You need to change course. Is your crew on the same page, or can't they stand the storm? Are they well prepared? The funny thing was that I started daydreaming during his metaphor, about sailing and relationships, and I think, after five minutes, I heard this voice in my daydream. And it was my dad, still talking about boats and sails, and I said, "Dad, that's enough." But I made myself laugh so hard. I love my dad. I was also a bit tired of training so the metaphor thing wasn't really getting through anymore.

The idea of writing this book gives me excitement. It gives me purpose. You know, the first book ever written was the Gutenberg Bible, in

Latin, in 1461. It was the first written book in Europe, besides the first writings, which were the Epic of Gilgamesh. It is a mythologized account of a historical figure, Gilgamesh, a ruler of the Sumerian city-state of Uruk, believed to have ruled sometime between 2700–2500 BC. It was written on clay tablets. Writing this book is also something for me to fall back on. Often, when you are on a journey like I am, with the Red Lions and Bloemendaal and my family, a lot of stuff happens. Later, when I look back to this period, I would like to have something in the form of this book: how we made it happen, and what mindset is needed to perform at your best level.

Beliefs

When you believe it, you'll see it. Your doing comes out of your being. When you are hateful, you'll do hateful acts. When you are angry, you'll do something out of that anger. I'm one that can project my anger onto objects, so I could smash my stick into the ground sometimes when I'm angry or frustrated. When you have love in your heart, people around you will notice this. When you are kind, you'll be forgiving and helpful towards the people around you. Being kind can be a choice when you are aware that you can control yourself.

Self-mastery is the ability to take control of your life, without being torn apart by feelings, urges, circumstances, etc.... In sports, it is much needed. Many players let themselves be led by the mistakes of others: bad referee decisions; the circumstances; the other team. You can often see a player totally flip when he gets a red card, or when he committed the fault or does a horrible tackle. At this instant, he didn't control himself enough and committed a fault. My two- year-old nephew, Jack, does this. He will cry when he's hungry or when he's tired. When he wants to play, he's full of excitement and smiles. Only when he really needs your help, he'll cry; or when he's crying in his bed, because he feels lonely, hungry, or thirsty. You never really know, until he stops crying, and then you know you did something good. I believe anything is possible.

I believe in the good of people. I believe hurt people hurt other people. Therefore, to break the cycle of this hurting, one must begin with themselves. Have you ever yelled at someone to "Be calm!!!" and he or she yelled back, "I am calm!!!" or "I'm not angry!!" while every part of his face is tensed and aggressive? That's just a funny situation. When you believe something, you will act upon it. Think about it. You and I believe that we have to go to school. We believe that we need a girlfriend or boyfriend in our lives. Then, when it gets serious, people will ask questions like, "What is the next step?" "Is it getting serious?" What does serious even mean? "Is she the woman of your life?"

What do you believe? Do you believe in God? Do you believe in life after death? Do you believe that we are just some coincidence? Do you believe that you and I are here for a purpose? Are we here to rule or to serve? To conquer or to share? What do you believe? What do I believe? I believe that one must always strive to do his best in order to create a better world. I believe that believing something can make you do big things. The reason I train every day is because I truly believe that the Red Lions can do something that has never been done before in Belgian hockey.

What do you believe? Write down 5 things you truly believe.

Limitless

Winners are made of blood, sweat, and data. This is the data we get after a game. There is a lot more specific data, but here is some of it to give you an idea of what one game is asking from us.

Eliud Kipchogee, is the world record holder in running a marathon in 2 hours, 1 minute, and 39 seconds. A normal human would be dead somewhere along the track if he would try such a time. But Eliud did it, because he believes that the human is limitless. And with that belief, he maybe hits a limit. But the inspiration that he is for the world is the most wonderful thing. By reaching and stretching for your own potential, you inspire others to do so as well.

Follow Up

You have to follow up. When I ever had a fight with my brother when I was young, my father would make us follow it up. It meant that when the emotions had calmed down, and being rational kicked in, we realised that hurting and fighting each other was of no good consequence. Our dad would make us come together and give each other a kiss, which was pretty awkward, I remember. I also remember really well that I was so upset about something that happened, and I had to go to my room. That was the sign you messed up. *Go to your room.* I remember being in my room, crying, and being very angry towards my brother, or my father because he didn't understand me. And then, suddenly, I didn't know what I was crying for anymore. But I remember saying to myself, "No, you have to stay angry!" And then I would ask, "But why stay angry?" I'd be frustrated because I felt I had the right to stay angry.

I had a discussion with Loïc Luypaert on the pitch. I was yelling, "Sort the structure out!" It was the last game against Holland before the World Cup. Our midfield was changing, and so we were completely out of structure. I yelled at him. Often, when I feel under pressure, I need structure. When I don't have structure, I start stressing out, and I yelled in this instance at Alexander Hendrickx, and Loïc came in between, yelling that I should not say anything. In the end, which was pretty funny to watch back on the computer, we were yelling at each other: "You shut up! No, you shut up! No, you shut up!!"

The next day, I was at Beerschot for training. And Shane Mcleod, our coach, came to me and said that I should talk to Loïc about the incident on the pitch, because he looked at it and saw that it didn't really look good. It looked pretty funny, actually. And then, just as he was talking about it, Loïck came in. What a coincidence. I started talking about the incident and what I was seeing and talking about on the pitch. We came to the conclusion that, indeed, we weren't in the right positions. But yelling at each other afterwards wasn't really helping. It's like saying something after a failure. You know you failed in this and that area. You know that yourself, but rubbing it in someone's face isn't really helpful. Helping each other resolve the situation, and talking about it afterwards in order to prevent it in the future, is a better idea. Having those crucial conversations with each other can really help you grow and develop the relationship with your teammates. Following up on an incident is needed. It takes courage and a certain level of integrity to face each other in those moments, and to talk openly and fairly towards each other.

When you open your mouth, you let the world know who you are.

Improve your communication skills. When you want to change the world, you'll need to speak your message well.

Chapter 11

Truth

Why?

Traveler, there is no path. You must make your path while you travel. It is the difference between a job and a calling. One night, I was feeling sort of down. I was tired of all the trainings: five days out of seven, two sessions a day; driving to Amsterdam on Friday to train with Bloemendaal, and playing the game on Sunday. I think it was a Saturday. I'm usually too tired to go out. So, most of the time, I'm alone. Then I like to read or watch YouTube.

So, I was feeling down, and then a voice in my head said, "Watch Oprah." Very funny. So I took my computer and opened YouTube. I searched Oprah, and there it was. Funny fact: December 2018, we lost the quarter final against India, and one of the comments of Michel Van Den Heuvel was that he didn't see a soul in our team. Probably more than half of our team forgot this already. But I wrote it down. I made a file on my computer, named *Soul Searching*. I haven't figured it all out, but a magical thing happens when you write something down that you would presumably find strange in the beginning.

It felt awkward to write it down in the beginning, because I had no clue what a soul was. What is a soul? What does it do? How can we find a soul? Deepak Chopra states the soul is the core of your being. It is eternal. It doesn't exist in space or time. It's a field of infinite possibilities, infinite creativity. It's your internal reference point which you should always be in touch.

Gary Zukav states that the soul is part of you that existed before you were born and that will exist after you die. It's the highest, most noble part of yourself that you can reach for.

Spirituality is the measure of how willing we are to allow grace – some power greater than ourselves – to enter our lives and guide us along our way.

163

Spirituality is a measure of how loving you are, how unconditionally accepting you are towards yourself and others. It is a living practice. You don't need to go to Italy, India or Bali to find your spirituality, although those places may be lovely to visit. It's right here in front of you. Right now. It's in every person you meet and every breath you take. It's everywhere you go, though you can't see it. You certainly can't buy it. And you won't find it in a book. None of these 'things' matter if you aren't being loving.

And so I came to that moment where my inner voice said, "Watch Oprah." And I looked for her, and there it was: SuperSoul Sessions. I found a pool where someone else had arrived: Oprah. And I started seeing everything that she was doing, and what she had done. I saw a video of Tom Brady, and he was saying that he found that a football game can be a spiritual event. Then I start feeling the adrenaline and excitement pumping; and I can get really excited. There was another video where Oprah explains the difference between a calling and a job, and that you do a job until you find your calling.

I think I found my calling. The way you can know your calling is by doing something, but you can't really explain why it is that you are doing it exactly. But people support you doing it, and you can't see yourself doing something else. What I had with hockey was that I also had a clear voice in my head, saying that this pitch isn't just a hockey pitch. It's a platform where you can show the world what you want. You can choose. It's up to you to find out how far you can go. When I'm playing and I'm making my actions, and I'm in my flow, that's where I feel really aligned with what I'm feeling on the inside. When I have those days, people will come up to me and say how amazing I played, or I could just feel that I inspired them. For me, I was just focusing on my game and doing the best I possibly could. Often, when we are in our best state, we don't immediately realise how much impact we have on others.

When you know your "why," you will find that the hard moments will be less hard–and there will be hard moments, whatever you do. Billionaires have hard moments, and poor people have hard moments. Some differ in looks, but as a human, you will have those moments. Unless you stiffen your vertebrae, those hard times will crush you, and you will perish. Your "why" is something where many of us don't dare to go. People stop with "what." *I want money, so I'll find a job.* "Why do you go to that job?" "Well, because of the money." The money is the result of what you do, not "why" you do it. Money is the reward. Start with "why." Simon Sinek has a great YouTube video about this. He also wrote a book about it: *Start with Why.*

Question: Why do you do what you do? Take the time to answer this one. You will find out, if you have never answered this question, that it can be hard to think about.

It Has Always Been You

Have you ever heard teammates say, "If we could just fix those losers, all would be better?" Well, they are one hundred percent wrong. Everything starts with you. You are the master of your faith, the captain of your soul. This kind of responsibility is something most of us don't take. Now, in the national team and Bloemendaal, when these teams don't function well, I take personal responsibility for the level of my team. You don't have to be the captain of the team to take a leading role. When you see an opportunity for your team to grow, you take it. When other team members don't see the benefit of this initiative, maybe you are in the wrong place, and you need to move on. When you take responsibility, you will find that you are the problem and the solution. You can be the light. You can be the difference. You have greatness in you! So, next time you have some of your negative, thoughtless thoughts, and you were not able to reflect on them before you spoke them into this world, think of what you said by asking these four questions:

1. Is it true?
2. Can I know that it is absolutely true? (Or does reality show that it can also be done differently?)
3. Who am I when I believe that thought?
4. Who am I when I am not able to believe that thought?

Happiness and effectiveness depends upon the kind of thoughts you think. It is absolutely impossible to be happy if you think unhappy thoughts. One of the wisest emperors of Rome was Marcus Aurelius, Roman Emperor, from 161 to 180. He was called the Philosopher. He said that *"a man's life is what his thoughts make of it."* If you put thoughts of fear into your mind, you will get thoughts of fear out of your mind. If you fill your mind with thoughts of resentment, resentment attitudes will emerge.

When you are in a business and are thinking that it will just be okay, and you are just going to work and go through the motions instead of putting in the hard work and manifesting greatness, your job and life itself will just be that unfulfilling place, and you'll notice that it's just not that. You'll have this nagging feeling that life is not what you thought it would be. When you want greatness in every part of your life, you don't settle. When you want to be better and are looking for ways to grow, to learn, and to stretch, and you are willing to go out of your comfort zone, life will be that wonderful place you have always dreamed of. But it's you! You have to make it happen.

Like me, for example, I always want to go for the best. In my case, it is writing history for my country by becoming the first Belgian team ever to be world champions. I always want to win, but I have lost many times. Often, I was ignorant. I didn't know I was doing stupid stuff. One of the things I had to learn was that everyone has different mindsets, different motives, and different buttons to push in order to step into their greatness. Now if I look back at some of the things I did, I say to myself, "Boy, you were really dumb." But within my knowledge and in my world, my behaviour seemed logical. It seemed like the right thing to do. I have a drive, and I just did it. I follow my gut and instincts. And usually, because I'm going so hard, I hit that wall pretty hard, crying and bleeding and sweating.

The transition from losing to learning is something most of us don't dare to make. It's hard to look at yourself and ask yourself what you want out of this life. Why am I here? What is my gift? What am I going to do for the rest of my life? What is it that I love to do? It's easy to blame circumstances. It's easy to blame the traffic for your bad mood. It's easy to blame the coach for your bad game. *It was the pitch. It's the weather. I just don't feel like it. My parents are having fights. I don't have the time. I'd rather go drinking with friends than work on myself. Drink the pain away. Take some drugs while I'm at it, because everyone is doing it.* People are being stuck at the same level without even knowing why, and not knowing that they have it all in their control. As it is written, *"The kingdom of God is within you."* – Luke 17:21.

There will be times when things aren't going to go so well, and times where you are filled with self-doubt and are in the grip of your inferiority complex. You'll say to yourself, "Why bother? Why go through all this? This is hard. I can't do it. I don't have it in me." It's important to then say to yourself that you have a very big "it" within you. You have the kingdom of God within you. Others call it a flame, or energy. Call it whatever you want, but we all have it. Sometimes I also need that wake up call to realise that every moment is an opportunity to change it all around. Every day is an opportunity. The next idea you have can be the opportunity that can change your life, but it's important to know that maybe there will be times when you don't have ideas.

What is it that you need to do then? Know that when you focus and work on your goals and dreams every day, for two hours, for the next five years, you will be a national expert after those five years. But it'll take you two hours, every day. Some people watch TV for three hours a day, and they spend two hours on their smartphone. But you can change the lives of millions of people. It all starts with you. Changed people change people. And that is the beauty of life. You can change. I hear people say you can't change. Well, they should go to a church or a prison, or to school. There are rooms full of people who are changing.

You can create a better and more fulfilling life. Last weekend, I went to the Inner Peace Conference in Amsterdam. It was about how to find your inner peace in this crazy world, and how to find some calmness; to know that if you want peace, you have to go into action within yourself. It starts with you. Max Strom, a yoga teacher who wrote the book, *A Life Worth Breathing,* teaches how to be aware of your breath and really focus on your breathing, which brings you in the present moment, and from then on, you can go into yourself. A funny fact is that the word, *aloha,* which is a word that people in Hawaii use to greet each other, means, *I breathe God with you.* Breath is so wonderful. Emotions and breath are highly connected. You probably can recall that when you are angry, you'll breathe more rapidly. When you're in deep sleep, you'll have a much calmer breath. So I meditate often, or generally focus on my breath often during games and trainings. When you go into yourself, meaning you observe your thoughts, feelings, or emotions, you are aware of what they are, and what that does for you. Mas Strom's belief (and science is on its way to proving it) that breathing, in the way he teaches it, can resolve anxiety and depression. It can also resolve past emotions or traumas that are locked in the body. As he says, *"We live in fear of terrorism, but in actuality, the most devastating terrorism comes from within us, as we sabotage ourselves."*

In what way are you sabotaging yourself? What feelings of resentment, grief, anger, or hate are you carrying within you that are hindering you from living your best life? While I'm doing Yin yoga on Saturday nights, which is kind of a meditation yoga where you rest in a pose for a couple of minutes while focusing on your breath, the first half an hour is a real struggle: My body gets warm, my head is fuzzy, and my thoughts are all around the shop. Trying to get my breath in a slower rhythm is hard, and then the anxiety and worry kicks in as well from time to time. I start reflecting on my life and why I'm doing this Yin yoga.

But then the teacher starts giving some tips, saying to take a deep, deep breath and then let it all out. After half an hour or so, I feel that my face is more relaxed, my breath is under control, and I'm floating with my mind over all the landscapes, hills, and cities I've been to. I can see myself there. I can see my thoughts and see everything getting connected. I can see my life from a distance and can see the path I travel. Then, when I walk out, I start to like the people a bit more around me, and I enjoy going through the streets of Amsterdam while enjoying the cold evening. Whereas normally I can look pretty tensed or tired because of my training programs, I feel my frustrations of the week are gone. Feelings of resentment and deeper heavier emotions are a bit lighter. I feel that everything is actually quite alright, and the options I have, or decisions I have to make, seem just a little bit easier. I immediately feel that I have to do this more. It gives me energy, and it feels great to calm down—to just sit and breathe; to enjoy breathing—and come to the conclusion that life starts with me, with my breath, and with my little flame inside me becoming a huge enormous flame.

Get It Done!

If men will not act for themselves, what will they do when the benefit of their actions is for all? To act in absolute freedom and at the same time know that responsibility is the price for freedom, is salvation.

Getting it done, getting this book done, getting it done to win that title, getting it done to rewrite history but not by choosing the easy route— I wrote a message to my dad once, where I said that I don't care how long it will take me. Maybe it will take my whole life. I will continue until I win that Olympic medal, and until I win that World Cup. Have that mindset to continue and focus until you get something done. What do you want to get done? Is it creating a happy family? Having that degree? Creating that business? When you visualize yourself with the end already in sight, seeing yourself there with what you want to have accomplished, and not stopping until your dream becomes a reality, that's freedom.

What do you want to get done? Know what it is that you truly want. Maybe, right now, what you think you want, you don't want at all. Maybe society or religion, or your family and friends, have influenced you to want what they want, while in fact, it has nothing to do with what your heart desires. Therefore, having the mindset of getting it done does not resonate with you because what you think you want is wrong. And then, when you die, having lived your life, you realise that you haven't lived at all. You lived your life for someone else.

The world needs people who, in their community, in their team, in their family, have the mindset to get it done. You won't find it in America, in Belgium, in the books you read, or in this book. You'll find it in *you*: a fire within that makes you want to get it done!

The Wright Brothers
Orville and Wilbur were two American aviators, engineers, inventors, and aviation pioneers, who are generally credited with inventing, building, and flying the world's first successful plane. There was a lot of competition to be the first to fly in that time. Being able to control an airplane could mean huge power for an army. It would change warfare completely. Of course, this was not the intent of the Wright brothers. They owned their own bicycle shop, where they started dreaming of flying in the air. They didn't have all the money. They didn't have the smartest engineers. They didn't have all the media attention. In France, they would be bullied. They were told they wouldn't be able to do it. They had willpower. They had a notebook. They experimented. They failed their way to success. The first powered flight was on December 17th, 1903: 37 metres in 12 seconds, at a speed of 10.9 km/h, and at approximately 3m above the ground.

Till the End

It's not over until I win. There is great energy I find in saying that you will continue your path until you win. Like in a game, you play until the last minute; whereas you stop playing after you're 2–0 down, when you, at that point, look at what you don't have and what the others do have. If the other team has two goals, and my team has no goals, that's a pretty sad situation, where a lot of people would give up on themselves. You can realise, however, that you have great players on your team. You have a fighting spirit within you. You have greatness within you. You can move mountains. You can have faith under all circumstances. You will not stop until your last breath, because you only live once in this life. *"A winner is a dreamer who never quits."*

A lot of times, I could have stopped playing the game, such as after losing the World Cup under 21 in India, where we were one of the favourites and were two goals up against France, with fifteen minutes to play. We conceded 3 goals in that last quarter, and we were out of the tournament. We were so close. If we would play them ten times, we would win nine times out of ten. I remember being devastated, which was also because I was involved in every goal. Of course, I wasn't the only one involved in the situations, but I felt that I failed big time, especially because we were so close and we were the better team.

When a team wins by playing exceptionally good hockey, I'll gladly shake their hand. But I had everything under control, so that broke me. I didn't notice, at that time, how much that affected me, especially with what my father was going through with his business as well (which I will explain further in the chapter, *Business Meets Sport*). A couple of months later, Philippe Goldberg, who was the coach of that U21 team, said, "I see now that you have finally come back from that defeat," meaning that the true me, the natural me, had returned. Most of us experience trauma and never come out of it. We turn to alcohol, drugs, or other addictive behaviour. I certainly had some of it. Hockey became my obsession. I was committed to achieving the best results possible with this game. I had decided to live for the game and give it everything I've got, and to go for that Olympic dream and achieve something that had never happened before in Belgian history. Something in me said that it was possible, so I went for it.

Soon, the first big success with the national team was reaching the final of the European championship, in Boom. The next devastation was the World Cup. Again, we played a team that we had beaten often. This time, it was Great Britain. We, again, finished first of our pool, and ended up against a team that were the underdogs. There's something about that underdog mindset that triggers teams to transcend their past performances. But if you're mindful that you need to have that same underdog mentality, as a favourite, nothing stands in your way. We lost that game and, afterwards, it was clear that we didn't reach our full potential in that game. Why that was, was maybe because of pressure, and because of the fear of losing. It might have been because we didn't expect the other team to be so good. We surely didn't manifest our greatness.

So, again, I was sick of this defeat, not because we lost but because we didn't play well. We did not reach our full potential. And that is as true in life as it is in business or in our relationships: our biggest frustration is that we cannot find the way to reach our full potential. At the end of our lives, we might regret the way we lived because of some fears or events, and that we could've followed our dreams and achieved our goals, but we didn't, because of fear of failure, or whatever. Franklin D. Roosevelt once said, *"The only thing we have to fear is fear itself."* And that's why sport is so amazing: When you listen to all the great athletes of their time, they all say that they did not have stress when they needed to perform for the gold medal. They changed that feeling into excitement for the unknown, and they conquered themselves.

The mind is the first battlefield you'll need to conquer. The thoughts you have often lead to certain actions: When you're hungry, your mind says to go and have that cookie. When you feel insecure in silent situations, your mind will say that maybe you should tell that joke to get rid of the awkwardness. Have you ever met up with someone you haven't seen for a long time, maybe a family member at an event or party, and you leave the party, but you didn't really have the feeling that you had a meaningful experience?

After that World Cup, we qualified ourselves against France, in a qualification tournament. So, again, we went from low to high. After we qualified for the Olympics, we failed again at the European championships by drawing against Ireland—again, a team that we would normally win against. Contentment is the biggest dream killer of humans. Then, after the European championships, our coach quit, and a new coach came in, ten months before the Olympics. We won silver at the Olympics, beating every team we were not able to beat in the last years: Australia, which was the current world champion; the Netherlands, which was the favourite to win gold; and Great Britain, which we had never beaten in every other big tournament in the past years. We made a quantum leap. It was hard, but it was worth it.

I remember sending a text, a couple of years ago, telling my dad that I didn't care if it took me ten years to finally win a medal. I would make the sacrifice to reach it, just to show that our small country is capable of great things. When you say to yourself that you will not quit, you take responsibility for yourself. When you take responsibility, others will take it as well. But it starts with you.

Lose Friends

When you are not losing friends, you are not growing. I used to think about friends I lost. I thought it was a bad thing for me, and that I should text them or call them, which I do often. But sometimes I do it out of a feeling of guilt or shame. Other times, I do it out of love, but there is a difference. Because of the fact that I had to train on Fridays and play a game on Sunday, I couldn't go out like others could. I couldn't live the student life like my other friends did: go out, have beers, and do stupid, fun stuff without really thinking about the consequences. When my friends would go skiing or go to the sea to have some fun, I would go to a training camp, or prepare for a tournament in the summer. And we couldn't have beers. We would have to go sleep on time, so we couldn't go to dinner parties or birthdays. I was just too tired, and I felt that I was very far from that social life.

When you are out of it for a while, you also can't really talk about the things they talk about. You don't really know who kissed who or who cheated on who, or who was able to do twelve ad fundums in one go, or who was in love with who. Lately, when we go out with the team to a bar or whatever, I also notice that when I drink, I can become very quiet. I can stand there without really feeling connected to the place. It might seem weird, but I don't really feel good in those places. I'd rather sit and have an intimate, one-on-one conversation. That's far more interesting to me. Although, when I feel comfortable and energetic, I can transform into a party animal. I think it had something to do with the fact that we just lost the playoffs with HC Bloemendaal and, therefore, I was feeling somewhat depressed. Again, we lost the semifinal after dominating the first game, losing the second game with two goals up, and losing in the last quarter, as the playoffs in Hoofdklasse are determined with the best of three. So, when you win two games, you go to the final. When you win the first but lose the second, or vice versa, the third game is decisive for who goes to the final.

Anyhow, where was I? Losing friends: I've lost friends, but there are some friends left where, if they call, or I call them, it seems like we have been connected all the time, even if we haven't had a lot of contact. I also don't really like birthdays. I would rather skip that day, but maybe that can change as well—you never know. Friends can also be destructive. When you have a dream or something you love doing, and it requires sacrifices, or it requires you to say no to certain things you don't want in your life anymore, friends can give you a lot of pressure to eventually lead you to doing what the group does.

When you are able to separate yourself from the pack and follow your own way, you can have a great, fulfilling and abundant life. I'm not saying that you won't need others. When you want to go fast, go alone; when you want to go far, go together. But then, find likeminded people who think like you and want the same things as you. Realising that your friends are holding you back, at some point in your life, will lead you to make hard decisions and to choose a different path. It will be hard. They will think you're weird or strange, or that you're a loner. But when you stick to your thing, they will soon find out that you were serious, and they'll respect you even more than before.

Look for Leaders

Read books. Go to seminars. Listen to successful people. Don't ask the waiter how to win gold at the Olympics. Find out how others became successful, and follow their strategy. Experiment. Read books. When you want to get to know somebody, ask what he reads and what he watches. Read about the Buddha. Read about Jesus. Read about Steven Spielberg and about Walt Disney. Read *Think and Grow Rich*, by Napoleon Hill. See inspiring movies. Do things you love and that give you energy—things that give you your life. Learn about those leaders. Learn to know yourself. Do whatever it takes. Have that commitment. Write down three goals that you want to achieve in this life, and hang them on your mirror where you can see them every day.

Because of the news, we see a lot of negative stuff. The world is to end soon, with great horror and unsolvable problems. Be aware of this. As our mind is filled with negativity every day, without us even realising it, be sure to also fill your mind with positive thoughts. I have a journal where I answer these questions every night:

• What have I given today? In what ways have I been a giver today?

- What did I learn today?
- How has today added to the quality of my life? How can I use today as an investment in my future?

And every morning:

- What am I **happy** about in my life right now? What about it makes me happy, and how does that make me feel?
- What am I **excited** about in my life right now? What about it makes me excited, and how does that make me feel?
- What am I **proud** of in my life right now? What about it makes me proud, and how does that make me feel?
- What am I **grateful** for in my life right now? What about it makes me grateful, and how does that make me feel?
- What am I **enjoying** most in my life right now? What about it am I enjoying, and how does that make me feel?
- What am I **committed** to in my life right now? What about it makes me committed, and how does that make me feel?
- Who do I **love**? Who loves me? How does that make me feel?

In this way, you choose your focus. It's easy to get up and the first thing you think about is your homework, or that meeting, or that presentation you need to do, or the bills you have to pay, or the bills you didn't pay. You have these thoughts that cause you a lot of stress immediately when you wake up. Instead of this, choose the thoughts you want to focus on, together with reading your goals of what it is you want. And while you are at it, answer these questions. In fact, what you can do, after you've answered them, is to do them with your family or your friends. Read every question, and give your little class three minutes per question, where they have to write down every answer, and if they want, they can share it with the group.

I did this once with my niece, Lauranne, and one of her best girlfriends, Britt, and with my grandmother, Bobi. All her grandchildren call her Bobi, after the little dog in Tintin. We named our grandfather, Baloo, after the big brown bear in the animation movie, *Jungle Book*, because our grandfather also had a big belly. After we did the questions, my grandmother said that if she were to write down something that made her happy today, it would be this moment, where two of her grandchildren asked deeper questions to each other, and thought about having a better life. As the saying goes, *"The quality of your life depends upon the quality of questions you ask yourself."*

- How do you define happiness? (Be specific.)
- Name/identify 2 or 3 of the most joyful adults that you know.
- Write down the names of your true friends.
- What is the most meaningful experience you've ever had?
- What is your code of ethics?
- If you find out in 15 minutes that you're dying, what would you regret in regard to what you have not done?
- What is the happiest period of time in your life so far, and what made it so?
- How can you improve your communication skills to have less conflict and more harmony?
- What is your mission in this life?
- How do you sabotage yourself in this life, preventing happiness and preventing having a meaningful life?

Don't Blame Circumstances

I was just driving home from my grandmother's, where we had dinner with some family. Some nephews and nieces were there. My stomach hurts from the nuts I ate—you know how, when you've had enough, but you keep eating. I knew I was going to regret it, but still, I went on. Earlier in the day, I had gone to the Heilig Hart Hospital, in Lier, where my mother had her exposition. She selected a whole segment of her work over the past years, and the hospital gives the opportunity for artists to have space in which to hang their creations. As a surprise, I called my Uncle Steven, who has a company, Make it Visible, which makes professional movies. My mother was very happy because she always wanted to make a video for her website. I was the interviewer, and I asked her lots of questions about why she painted, and about what goals and dreams she still has. I could feel that talking about this made her very happy, as with this exposition, she has a new start for the future.

With my grandmother, I had a nice talk with my nephew, and my niece, who is pregnant. They stayed a little later than the others, and we started having conversations about everything—about our first loves, about marriage, about feeling depressed, about our most meaningful experiences—a moment and space where we could just talk. I think that is something people miss: just talking, without judging; talking about how you feel. One of the biggest regrets people have is not expressing their genuine feelings. When I drive home in my car, I often put on YouTube videos (Les Brown, Jim Rohn, Oprah...) that are motivational or inspirational. Because I'm in the car quite often, and know most of the songs already, these videos are sometimes music to my ears. It's like a driving classroom. I learn the psychology of wealth in my car, which is pretty nice.

One of the things that made a new groove in my brain was something Jim Rohn (an American author, entrepreneur, and motivational speaker) said in one of his videos. There are four major lessons to learn in life. Learn how to handle the winters. Winters are coming—winters where you can't figure it out; winters where it all goes smack; winters where it won't work, because you don't have any money and you have a broken heart. You will have all kinds of winters— economic winters, social winters, and personal winters—where you don't have any people who say they need you; you don't get any birthday wishes; you don't get any postcards; your heart is smashed in a thousand pieces; and the nights seem unusually long. All this is hard and cold, and you have all had a few of these moments. But disappointments are going to come, and they are a part of life.

That's not the question, though. The question is, how do you handle it? How do you handle the cold circumstances? How do you handle the rain? How do you fix the broken heart? How do you earn that higher income? How do you handle the downtimes? You can't get rid of winter. It's going to come every time, after fall. You can't erase it off your calendar, but here's what you can do: You can get stronger, you can get wiser, and you can get better. The winters won't change, but you can. That's how life changes for you. When it was hard, I wished it was easy. When it was winter, I wished it was summer. When it was easy, I wished it was hard. I didn't know how it worked, but then this video made it clear in my mind how to think about it. It continues.

Don't wish it was easier; wish you were better. Don't wish for less problems; wish for more skills. Don't wish for less challenges; wish for more wisdom. That's the key. The second lesson is to learn how to take advantage of spring. Life is short. You'll only have a couple of springs. Lesson three is to learn how to protect your crops all summer, because you'll want to have them. Lesson four is to learn how to reap without complaint. Don't complain. Accept full responsibility. That's where you can see if someone is mature or not. See what they say after a defeat. See who they blame or what they blame, and look for those who take full responsibility for the result.

Take the initiative!!
Don't wait for things to happen….

MAKE THEM HAPPEN, damn it!

It comes from the inside.

Chapter What Now

World Champions

Okay, I'll have to be honest: It has been one week after the World Cup, and I feel a need to write. Emotions are becoming bigger and stronger. We started the game off well against Canada. We took the lead with two goals. But, in the third quarter, things started to get a bit messy, and the flow was gone. I must admit that I was feeling a bit lost. I started thinking too much about the tournament, about the game, and I made more mistakes. I took too much responsibility for the mistakes I made and the consequences. The danger is that I get paralyzed and don't play and don't communicate. Jamie Dwyer once said that when things are not going your way, there are three things you can do:

- Communicate
- Work hard
- Play simple

These three things can make you focus again, because you are, as a player, part of the World Cup team. We have big dreams. We want to win it for the first time in the history of Belgium. To climb a mountain, it starts with the first step, the preparation, and what you put in your backpack. We have had a good preparation. We are all fit. We worked hard. We are all skillful. We don't have any weak links. I do feel that we have a permanent investment in each other because we are together a lot.

The interactions we have are crucial. How we handle them is critical, as well as how we grow as individuals. In this instance, I start doubting or judging other people and how they are growing. I believe that when you give the right example, it will inspire others to do the same. Therefore, it is important to be aware of what you think, say, and feel, and how you communicate. Everybody did their utmost best to be here. And everybody is different. Maybe some had to work harder. Some had more pain. Some had to overcome more obstacles. Some had more personal struggles. You don't know. You do your best and God does the rest.

What's On My Mind?

I'm having a good day. I feel energised. I think one of the reasons I'm writing again is that it makes you present. It allows you to explore who you are. It's a way to revisit the past. As I am here, playing for the World Cup, I think a lot about all the other tournaments I played in, and I think about what moments were decisive and which were not. I think about the things I did that made me successful, and about the things that made the team successful. Writing also makes you connect with the present. It's dangerous to constantly think in the past or be busy with the future. In doing so, I lose connection with the team and with the people around me, and I stop enjoying things and I lose energy. It's important in this environment to be of high energy, yet to be calm and determined. Writing makes you map out the future. I feel it is a way to control yourself in the future, no matter what may come; and no matter how bad it is, or how bad it gets, I am going to make it.

Injury

It is the third of December, 2018. We are against India during a sprint forward with the ball, launching an attack. From the minute it happened, I knew it was over. I ran to the sideline because I wanted Gauthier coming on so he could defend as India took the ball, to start a counterattack. I walked to the back of the dugout and threw my stick against the wall while cursing! I was so angry. First, I was angry; then I felt broken. My life flashed before my eyes: all the things I had done, all the sacrifices, all the trainings, the solitude, the failures, and all the setbacks that I overcame.

The tears started rolling. I realised that it was done. Over. Julien Rysman, our physio person, came to me and tried to console me. He tried convincing me I would come back. But I said that it was done. He tried to convince me that it would go better, but I knew it was over. So much emotion came out of me. I've cried, but never like this. Every decision I made to get here—and the people who helped me—was it all for nothing? I broke down several times. In the hotel, I decided to go back home. I felt like a failure again.

After two days, I was back home, figuring out what to do. Michiel Sleebus was making a presentation for his class, about the Red Lions, in first grade. His parents asked if I could make a video for his presentation. I planned to make it after the game against India, because there would be 18,000 people in the stadium. But then the injury happened, and I forgot about it, so I made it in my room. Also, because of the injury, my world was turned upside down, so the video wasn't as glamorous as I hoped it would be. Then an idea popped in my head: What if I just go and surprise him at his school, and pop up during his presentation? They would never expect it because the kids think I'm still in India for the World Cup.

In the meantime, I was reading the book, by Gaus Gopar Dal, about an Indian monk who became famous with his YouTube video, *Why Worry?* His book, *Life's Amazing Secrets: How to Find Balance and Purpose in Your Life*, helped me a lot while going through this setback. It talks about how to conquer your daily battles, align yourself with your purpose, and win at life.

Lost and Found

Faith is the substance for things hoped for, and the evidence of things not seen.

You have to have a tremendous work ethic, but you also have to have faith. In the beginning, you hope something will just pop up. When I was a young boy, I wrote down in one of my friend's books that I wanted to be a pro athlete. I remember that I was watching the Belgian Olympic Delegation on the television, and I was seeing that there wasn't any successful Belgian team. Sure, we had athletes, but not a successful team. It's funny how it goes that when you ask or question something, you somehow attract it into your life. It's like life will present the opportunity to you to do something about it. And in doing so, and by doing it, it makes you humble. It makes you, once you succeed in it, hungry for more things you want to attract into your life. And you become unstoppable.

Imagination is everything. It's the preview to life's coming attraction. Imagination is the evidence of things not seen. You are the only one who can see it. Your imagination is actually God giving you a preview of a coming attraction that he has for you. The moment you don't believe in your imagination, you neglect what God has in store for you.

You have not, because you ask not.

The day of the India game, I got up with a bad feeling. I had a nightmare. The dream was that Felix Denayer would get very mad at the team. The team would not go. Everybody would get angry. I got up and told Felix that I dreamed about him. Thomas also had a bad dream, where Felix said to him that he needed to stop playing hockey. And during the game, Felix did get mad. So that was a funny experience.

A man without a vision shall parish.

I'm sick and tired of myself. And I am willing to do everything it takes to get there.

I'm just free riding my feelings, and it's tough.

But I feel life has something more in store for me. Pain is temporary. It will go away. I talked to the team, explaining that I would fly home tomorrow or Wednesday. The moment I had to talk to the team, I already had trouble controlling my emotions. Ned tapped me on the back, saying it would be alright. Vic also gave me a good tap on the leg, consoling me. And then I started speaking, straight from the heart, saying that life is tough sometimes. You work hard for something, you get up every day for it, and you challenge yourself.

To have it taken away so suddenly, is tough; but that's how life goes. Don't think you are the only one. I will be home, but I will be thinking about this team. I always think about this team—when I'm home, when I'm in the car—I always think about this team and how to make it better. I go in overthinking mode. I think about how to make myself better, to find ways to improve. We are really close to becoming the world's best team so that we can shatter the belief that this small country can't create the best team in the world. We can shatter the belief of the doctor who once said that Belgium is worth nothing anymore, and that it is broken.

On the plane back to Belgium, I got a note from someone who learned that I had been injured during the World Cup. He wrote down: *"Nothing is that broken that it cannot be fixed."* And that is true. Something that seems negative now, will become your biggest strength some other day. You have to keep going, even if you are crawling. Keep moving forward. It is not the country that is broken. It is the people in the country who need inspiration and to believe again in their goals and dreams. The richest place in the world is the graveyard, where all the best ideas and dreams are buried because people never had the courage to go after them. And you have a great potential. We are so close, and I believe that this team is capable of doing it.

This injury came out of the blue. I'm now in London, writing this book with Raymond, a *New York Times* bestselling author. My brother, Sander, works and lives in London. My purpose for being here is to finish my book. The reason I'm writing this book is to teach you how to use a winning mindset to become the world's best, and how to overcome failure, setbacks, and fears, to achieve your goals and dreams. And now I'm here, having one of my biggest setbacks. *Every setback is a setup for a comeback.*

All types of fears come up. Will I come back stronger? Will I have the strength to come back? I don't have the energy. Should I start a study? I'm frustrated, and lonely. I gave everything for this game. I saw Julien, a good friend of mine. He had to come back from New York where he studies. His visa suddenly got blocked because of some new law the Trump administration pushed through. He had to drop everything and come back to Belgium. Like me, he was forced to quit his dream—his life. It's funny how life goes. People have the same kinds of setbacks, in different environments. Life will catch you from the blind side.

I will come back stronger. I will not quit. I will never quit. I wouldn't have quit if I didn't get injured. So why let something I couldn't control determine my destiny? I control my destiny, and I make it happen. I can do it. And so can you. See your goal, and go for it, and don't quit. Don't stop. You can do it. You are closer than you think!

School Dream

I had a dream where I would go back to school and do it all over again. And this time, I would know what I had to do and how to not make all the same mistakes. The dream starts really good, but then everything starts to come back—being late, forgetting my notes, not knowing there is a big test coming up, feeling ashamed and embarrassed, teachers being angry—it ends up being a nightmare. One of the things that were on my list to do was going back to school and meeting my math teacher again. When I wanted to go to my last year, and change from economics and math to economics and languages, so I wouldn't have to do the math hours and could focus more on my trainings from hockey, it came down to me doing an exam, which my math teacher would make, and I would have to learn in the summer. I didn't study so well for the exam, because I was thinking that I wasn't going to do this anymore anyhow.

And I had a summer full of hockey and holidays. I was convinced I could go to the last year, but I did the exam and failed. Okay. My bad. But I just couldn't do math anymore. I was so traumatised by all the negativity around it that I just couldn't study anymore. I loved playing hockey and being outside, not studying inside for a math teacher I hated, at that time. It was just horrible. When I failed the exam, the teacher, who had the final say on letting me go to the last year, and giving me the opportunity of changing classes, wrote on my final report: *"Emmanuël isn't capable of doing the last year."* She gave me a C-attest, which means she decided on her own that I should do my year over. She wrote that I wasn't able to do it, and that I couldn't do it. She literally wrote it down—wrote down that I couldn't do it.

Anyway, there are, of course, two stories. Hockey wasn't that known, so they didn't take my story so seriously about the hockey, which made it even harder for me because I felt lonely in my belief that it was something real.

I had to go back, and I went back last week. I got to know that there would be a New Year's drink on a certain evening, and it would be possible to see the math teacher, as she retired a year ago. I entered the school again, and I was shaking but confident. This was the school I had this traumatising experience with. Now, it is seven years later. There were maybe fifty teachers and, of course, Joost Van de Pontseele was there. Mister Lefevre and Mister Rotthier were there as well. It was really nice to see them all again. And then there she was—my math teacher. I said I dreamed about being back here. And now I was. I was afraid of doing it, but I did it. I explained the whole thing and, of course, she didn't remember it that well (she says). But I had to close the cycle, explaining that it was blocking a lot of energy, and I needed to get rid of it by seeing her and talking about it. And so, I managed to finish off my hockey story with a title. And I closed the story with my school. It feels like a new start.

Comeback

In order to come back, you need a good mentality and positivity to believe in your comeback, and to believe that you will achieve your dream. There will be a lot of lonely, awkward moments in the gym, where you will have to do exercises you wouldn't do normally. There you have it again that you will be put outside your comfort zone. And that is exactly where you need to be when you want to grow. Growth takes place when you get knocked down. People often see setbacks and challenges as a negative thing. But imagine that everything you are going through is exactly what you need to get what you want. Lars is helping me with my revalidation. You meet these people who are experts in their field, and they help others to achieve their dream. Isn't that magical? When you are struggling, know that it is that struggle that you need to get through to get to the other side. Don't quit. Never quit. There is always a way. Winners train. Losers complain.

Warning:
EYE OPENER

—

These questions, I did with Maarten and Govert. I had an urge to know what is out there in the world for a guy like me with my personality and my hockey experience. I was a bit worried that when the hockey would stop, I would not know where to go. These questions, I sent to thirty to forty people I know, and the answers were quite nice to hear. It's a nice thing to do to become more self-aware.

Sparrow Questions

Ask these questions of 10–15 people you know:

1. What do you like about me when we are working together or just being together?
2. What do you find are my qualities?
3. What pitfalls do you want to warn me about?
4. What type of role/function do you see me doing?

These are the Sparrow questions I did with Goverth Ho and Maarten Frowein. I got to know them at Bloemendaal. They started to help top sporters who needed guidance with the transition from sport to work. I sent this to my teams, family, and friends, and it's actually a confidence builder, because others see things in you that you didn't realise before. And when everyone says it, it is quite nice, because it makes it real.

BAM!

The END

Is just a new beginning.